UNDERSTANDING
MODERN
Spirituality

UNDERSTANDING
MODERN

Spirituality

An exploration of your soul and higher truths

INNA SEGAL

ROCKPOOL

A Rockpool book
PO Box 252
Summer Hill
NSW 2130
Australia

rockpoolpublishing.com
Follow us! **f** 🄾 rockpoolpublishing
Tag your images with #rockpoolpublishing

ISBN: 9781922785121

Published in 2023 by Rockpool Publishing
Copyright text © Inna Segal 2023
Copyright design © Rockpool Publishing 2023

Images from Shutterstock

Design and typesetting by Sara Lindberg, Rockpool Publishing
Edited by Brooke Halliwell

 A catalogue record for this
book is available from the
National Library of Australia

Printed and bound in China
10 9 8 7 6 5 4 3 2 1

Contents

About the author

Inna is an internationally recognised healer, teacher, professional speaker, author and pioneer in the field of energy medicine and human consciousness. By intuitive means, she can 'see' illness and blocks in a person's body, explain what is occurring, and guide people through self-healing processes. However, her focus is not just to help a person heal physically but to also help them reconnect to their spiritual divine nature and understand deeper aspects of evolution.

When Inna was a teenager, she suffered from severe back pain, anxiety and a skin disorder. In an incredible twist of fate, while meditating, Inna was able to receive help from the divine source and unlock her ability to intuitively see into her body. By asking pertinent questions she was able to discover the root of her pain, release heavy energies and emotions and heal herself. This experience awakened her intuitive abilities to see what is happening in other people's body's and inner lives.

She is able to teach her students how to understand the symbolic ways that their body and soul communicate through metaphors, images, feelings, memories, colours, sensations, thoughts and symbols.

Inna Segal is the award-winning best-selling author of *The Secret Language of Your Body: The Essential Guide to Health and Wellness*, *Heal Yourself Reading Cards* and *Mystical Healing Reading Cards*.

Inna has also created a variety of helpful healing audios and in-depth online programs. Her mission is to help people to awaken their inner life and step onto their true path of wellness, creativity, and to acknowledge their gifts and abilities that their spirit has brought to them.

Her books, cards and events (both live and online) are based on deep ancient wisdom, combined with a modern understanding of what we need right now to be our best selves, and the processes which allow us to grow and expand in a safe, profound and lasting manner.

Her passion is to help people understand the hidden mysteries of our existence – in particular, where we came from, where we are at the present moment, and where we are going in our future incarnations.

She deeply believes that we have to become more conscious of spiritual realities, which help us to understand the most progressive ways to live.

Find her at innasegal.com or on facebook.com/InnaSegalAuthor

Introduction

Whenwethinkdeeply,wehave an opportunity to connect the pieces of our life in a profound and inspired way. My intention with this book is to encourage you to stretch your mind like never before. To inspire you to question your life, your education and the understanding of who you believe yourself to be.

I strongly feel that when we are courageous enough to ask some big questions and are not afraid to put in some effort to grow, that our life truly unfolds. At the same time, I believe we must create a strong foundation for our inner life, which can hold us up in any challenging situation we may encounter.

This book started with me sharing many of my discoveries on social media. I received profound responses and decided to collate those sharings into a short book where I explore many themes of life, death, soul and spirit and examine numerous old, outdated, ambiguous teachings that have dominated the New Age industry. Feel free to read it from cover to cover or to flip through the book and see what takes your interest. Some of the topics relate to everyday life and others invite you to think, research and grow.

I challenge you to take your time to contemplate some of the ideas presented, work with the various processes and discover your own truth.

So often people say that truth is simple, yet I would beg to differ. I feel that this belief keeps people on the surface, going round and round in circles and never truly understanding the deeper mysteries of existence.

How can higher truth be simple? We only have to look at the physical body and all the processes that science has discovered about it to recognise how complex we are. Imagine all the things that science doesn't know and can't perceive – including our energy bodies, our soul and spirit, let alone answer questions of where we came from, where we are now in the evolution of humanity and where we are going.

This book is not here to answer all these questions, as that would require many long volumes of work. Instead I am here to shake you out of any idleness and dare you to go on a fearless search towards your own inner awakening, while offering you powerful healing tools in the process.

I have broken up the various topics into sections in order to give you an overview of what you will discover in this book.

The bigger picture looks at how we can start to think and see life from a new perspective.

Your subtle bodies dives into some powerful understandings of the astral, etheric and ego bodies.

Celestial beings and a cosmic exploration discusses the role that God and the hierarchy of angelic and divine beings play in our evolution.

Your soul, karma and the spiritual realm investigates some pretty big topics including multiple earth incarnations and why we need to learn what happens in the spiritual realms after we die, while we are still here on earth.

Spiritual awakening, intuition and inner mastery examines how you can face your shadow, work with your feelings, and deepen your path towards spiritual evolution.

Ancestral healing, sexuality, and what's next uncovers how our family and ancestors impact our wellbeing and our lives. We also delve into certain connections between sexuality and intuition.

The last part of this book offers you transformational processes for physical, emotional and ancestral healing – I encourage you to keep coming back to this section over and over again, allowing yourself to truly tune in and work deeply on your inner wellbeing.

HOW TEACHABLE ARE YOU?

Your willingness to learn and accept change determines how teachable you are. For you to gain the most out of this book or any experience, your desire to learn, your willingness to apply what you learn and change things in your life must be extraordinarily high! Your willingness to let go of judgements, doubts, negativity and self-sabotage must also be high. Your desire to transform your life, let go of limitations, pain, sickness and what does not work must be higher than your desire to hold on to what you know. The question is how tired are you of going round and round in circles?

WHAT CAN HOLD YOU BACK?

Every time you have a thought like 'I already know this', 'I've heard it before', 'this doesn't apply to me', 'I can't see myself doing this' and so on, your ability to learn diminishes enormously and at this point you may become virtually unteachable without realising it.

It's easy to say that you already know a potentially helpful concept; however, unless you are applying what you know in your life and seeing real results, you don't really know it.

Wisdom is being conscious of what you know and what you know you don't know. As Albert Einstein said, 'The more I learn the more I realise how much I don't know.'

Your inner foundation becomes unwavering when you are willing to step out of your comfort zone and constantly put into practice what you know has the potential to move you forward.

To keep your agreements with yourself and others is one of the most profound building blocks to creating steadfastness, living your purpose and becoming a trustworthy person.

I ask that you use this book as an opportunity to learn, question, think into new understandings and create change.

Here are some questions you may like to meditate on. Your willingness to participate could be high, medium or low. Be honest. This allows you to review your motivation as well as your capacity to take massive action in order to create change.

★ What is my willingness to learn? For instance, how willing are you to give up your most favourite things, for example: money, time, watching TV, judgement, procrastination, eating sugary food, holidays and/or shopping in order to learn something new or to work with the processes in this book?

★ What is my openness to learning something new and different to what I presently believe and to open my mind and heart to it before I judge it or discard it? For instance, if you read something that doesn't make complete sense to you or is asking for you to research the higher worlds, are you open to exploring and researching it?

★ What is my willingness to delve into a more eternal type of thinking? This type of thinking is connected to the bigger picture of life. Are you willing to think about angels, archangels, the higher worlds, sleep and karma?

★ What is my willingness to change, even if this change means giving up what I know and what I am comfortable with? Are you willing to face your fear of something new and the possibility that it may change not only how you think but how you live?

★ What is my willingness to take responsibility for my learning and not blame someone else when I don't get what I think I want? At times people feel that if they do everything right, they should have whatever they want, but that's not how life or destiny works. Sometimes we get the experiences that we need to learn from, even if we don't want them. When we take responsibility we have the capacity to discover a helpful point of view and take steps forward in our life and evolution.

The answers to these questions will determine how much you are willing to grow, stretch and challenge yourself.

THE BIGGER
PICTURE

A new kind of happiness

We are all sold a dream that says happiness equals success. And to be successful you have to be happy.

Yet as one grows and learns, there is a realisation that happiness doesn't necessarily offer you a great deal of depth and growth. And that maybe to be happy we have to close our eyes, ears and hearts to our environment.

When you see and feel what is happening in the world as well as dealing with your own inner and outer challenges you are not necessarily happy. Yet as you do the work and grow, an inner depth and richness develops in you and you realise that you can transform many aspects of your own closure, numbness, pain, anger and fear and that through your own inner effort you can become a helpful, compassionate person.

Maybe underneath the idea of just getting what we want as soon as we want it, there lies a different type of feeling where we can understand and develop true openness of heart and compassion, not only as a feeling for our selves but as a deed that also contributes to others. And maybe through our selfless actions a new type of more subtle richness appears within us, one that awakens a feeling of awe for all the divine forces and all the beings on this planet that have created the possibilities we have. Perhaps this leads us to a new kind of happiness – one full of wonder, admiration and amazement.

The question is: what do we do with what shows up in our reality?

Do we spend most of our lives feeding the fear, pain, hurt, anger and worry?

Do we only focus on what we want, despite how it impacts others, so that we can fulfil our own aspirations and desires, or do we observe what is happening within us and around us and choose to ask some big questions, contemplate, learn, grow and more than anything, act from a place of gifting something new to others?

In that possibility we can discover a different aspect of fulfilment ...

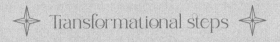

✦ Transformational steps ✦

For the next 24 hours examine your thinking. Are you passively yearning for someone to give you a sense of happiness without any effort? Or are you actively working on your thinking in a way that helps you to feel energised, enlivened and useful?

Are your feelings constantly up and down based on what is occurring in the outer world? Can you take some time to become a master of your feelings by recognising that how you think about yourself, your life and the outside world impacts how you feel?

Try this activity: Slow down your breathing and place your hands on your heart. Ask: 'What am I feeling in this moment?' If the feeling is numb or empty, imagine that this empty feeling has a colour and a shape. What colour is it? What shape? Visualise a purple fire in front of you. Take out any dense colours and shapes from your heart and place them into the purple fire. Concentrate on letting go of your fears and limitations. Now focus on these thoughts: 'How can I be of service to my family, my community, the world?' Imagine doing something helpful for others that is meaningful to you. Feel the gratitude from that person or the community. Imbue yourself with this new feeling of happiness.

In the next seven days consciously do something that is meaningful to you and others. It can be as small as smiling at someone in a shop, or as big as helping people in a community or the world change their thinking, feelings and lives.

Our education

From early on in life so many of us have been brainwashed into believing that there is nothing more than the material world and we are just a physical body, a machine, that has a tendency to get sick and will eventually perish.

If we are fortunate enough to be shown that we are spiritual beings, in the depth of our unconscious we may still hold old theories and limitations, which are connected to our education.

For example, we are either too afraid to learn the deeper truth about the spiritual aspects of ourselves and the spiritual world or we attempt to convince ourselves and others that everything is simply a reflection of the physical reality! Yet to truly learn about the higher worlds we have to be extremely teachable and willing to let go of our old concepts. We have to ask questions and enter into active thinking about the super-sensible realities.

However, in our current culture of quick fix we have been taught to stay on the surface and not commit to any deep discoveries unless it has the word science attached to it. In fact, we have even been sold on the idea that spiritual truths and wisdom are easy and do not require much investigation or inner work.

Unfortunately, science only investigates what is seen and can be dissected and studied in its physical form. Occasionally quantum physics comes along and proves that everything is energy, yet I always wonder why most people don't ask questions like, 'What is energy and where does it come from?'

The big picture of who we are, how we got here and what our real soul journey is, has been shrouded in confusion, misunderstanding and lots of theories that lack connective tissues of how we really came about, who helped us, how, where and when the physical body developed and what energy bodies are we made up of and why? What is our soul, and what is its role and so on?

We need to develop the courage to start asking deeper questions and making the time to discover some of the answers.

In this book, I ask you to contemplate these topics from different angles. I remember myself at six. One day some thoughts planted themselves into my mind: where did I come from? What is death? Is it the end of my life as I know it? Who is God? Even at that tender age, I felt curious about what it means to be a human. I asked my mum, who was busy cleaning the house. She gave me an unsatisfying, generalised answer. I made a decision to find people who knew more than her, whether it was through meeting them and asking direct questions or through books. Somewhere in my young mind I felt that by understanding those questions, I would gain inner strength and discover my purpose.

That curiosity has never left me. I have not stopped asking questions and learning from those who have brought amazing wisdom to this planet. I have read sacred texts from a variety of religious denominations as well as esoteric or hidden writings which contain profound spiritual wisdom. I have learned from eastern gurus, health specialists and multiple life experts. I've looked to painters and sculptors who brought sacred art to us. I've listened to musicians who claim they can hear angelic voices. I have met and read countless books by authors who have had extra sensory experiences. I have studied playwrights who brought mystical ideas to the world. I explored the writings of western initiates. I have been a student of many wise teachers who have shared with me about the soul, the spirit and the stars, the universe and our destiny.

Each time I discovered a piece of wisdom, I would sit with it, meditate on it, explore how I could apply it and tune into how it impacted my soul. When I felt uplifted, even if I'd had resistance, I would dig deeper. If the exploration made me feel drained, stuck, frustrated, chaotic and confused I would put it aside, ask my inner being why it wasn't resonating and open myself to discovering more details. I believe that we need to have open-mindedness as well as discernment. We need to have the courage to ask questions and find pieces that fit and make our souls more enlivened.

In this book, I ask many questions and encourage you to find the pieces that will allow you to make more sense of your life and bring more depth and vitality into your soul. Deep thinking requires you to go beyond the obvious, it doesn't ask you to believe based on faith, it asks you to explore and discover.

✦ Transformational steps ✦

Give yourself permission to go deeper and ask questions about who you are, where you came from and where you are going. Take time to contemplate this on a personal level of your family, as well as on a universal level of humanity.

When focusing on the bigger pictures it can be incredibly uplifting to sit with feelings of awe.

Consciously seek out people, groups, books or teachings that can help you start to explore deeper questions. There are many points of view on truth. It's time to discover more about what speaks to you.

New ways of thinking!

The more I learn about the complexity of who we are the more in awe I am. To learn to think in new ways creates a totally different experience of life.

Often when I say this people comprehend it as thinking positively about something which was previously perceived as negative. Yet I'm talking about having thoughts such as:

★ What really happens when I fall asleep?

★ Is sleep just a physical phenomenon or do I actually go back through all my lives when I sleep?

★ Do I meet certain higher angelic beings when I sleep or is the depth of my relationship with them based on what I have done during this day to build that connection through my thoughts, feelings, words and actions?

★ Why do some people have an amazing revitalising sleep and others wake up even more tired?

★ Which aspects of my being stay in bed when I sleep and which go into the cosmos?

★ If I understood the importance of sleep and what truly happens, would I change how I live and think about things during the day and what I invest my time into?

Imagine how different your life would be if you spent significant time each day entering into and contemplating the mysteries of sleep, your higher bodies and the higher beings.

After all, the saying 'we become what we think about most of the time' rings true. So what do you think about most of the time?

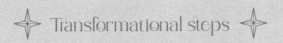

✦ Transformational steps ✦

Grab a journal and give yourself five minutes. Write down as many new thoughts or questions as you can that you rarely or never contemplate. At the end ask yourself: how would my life transform if I gave more time to deeper contemplation, as opposed to just thoughts of survival?

Place your hands over your heart. Imagine that your heart is growing and expanding in love and in its capacity to receive deeper insights. Imagine that these insights are like various colours of the rainbow with many shades. Focus on any colour, for example, green. Tune into the various tones of green, emerald, jade and so on. Sense the subtle difference in how those colours make you feel.

For the next 14 days take small, medium or large actions that enhance your life and understanding of your inner world. This could be anything from taking five minutes to meditate, having a deeper discussion with a work colleague or doing something super loving to someone, just because you want to. The key is that each action must be done consciously.

Is it all just physical?

So often I have read articles and posts on social media about how toxic things, which are everywhere and pretty much in everything, affect and break down our physical bodies.

Obviously, our physical bodies are important. It's just that if we start to focus only on the physical and all the fear that is around almost anything we do, we will become stuck, limited, confused and afraid.

As everything in our present world has a potentially damaging element in it, we can spend so much of our precious time obsessing about the fact that our food, water, air, make-up, hair products, face and body products are all full of chemicals. And if we delve even deeper we would most likely find that many companies who put organic stickers on their products are still hiding some toxic elements.

If we are honest even organic food no longer has the nutrients we need, our house can be mouldy, or we can spend too much time watching TV, working with technology and being affected by 5G, let alone whatever else is zapping us. We can be super strict and protective, drinking pure water, eating biodynamic food, living in the forest and then one day, visit a friend and drink their contaminated water and get super sick or be run over by a car while crossing the road in a town where there are hardly any cars or fumes. It's never-ending.

Yet what we often forget is that we only have our physical bodies for a short time and they offer us a possibility to grow and to discover who we are! Our constant focus on the physical will eventually disappear when we no longer have a physical body.

Imagine spending all your life focusing only on keeping the physical body healthy and then entering the spiritual worlds and being asked what aspects of yourself you developed that were beyond the physical. Would you feel a bit lost?

Having struggled with my own physical challenges I went through a time where I tried to be as pure as possible with what I ate, drank and put on my body. Eventually, I recognised that it can become a vicious cycle. At one point I felt it was a full-time job just to keep my physical body going, through non-stop detoxing, fasting, juicing and doing countless other procedures. What actually brought me to a new realisation was that after all the effort I had put in, I not only didn't feel better, but I actually felt considerably worse, malnourished and developed an extra physical problem I didn't have when I started. This doesn't mean that I don't believe in living healthy, because I certainly do, I just know how easy it is to become obsessively focused on the physical body and spend all your time, energy and money on it.

Yet if you enter the spiritual world with very little of the eternal aspects of self-knowledge and refinement then I believe you are more likely to end up with a weak physical body in your next incarnation and have a higher likelihood of being born into a difficult environment. If you don't deepen your capacity to think, you are also likely to be born with a weakened mind, with lots of anxiety and a diminished capacity to deal with life's challenges.

I mean, even now, if you look around, how many more kids are being born sick or weak and are diagnosed with all sorts of disorders by the time they are seven?

This occurs when we don't understand that the physical body is a vehicle that gives our soul the possibility to transform and redeem different facets of our shadow aspects and thus awaken our higher faculties.

The obsessive focus on the physical can easily take over our lives, especially if we have ailments. I've seen people who only eat organic food, sleep on organic mattresses, have air purifiers, eat vegan diets and take countless supplements become sicker than the people who smoke, drink and eat the unhealthiest food you can imagine. I am not encouraging the latter. I just want to bring attention to the fact that we have to look deeper!

I've seen people pedantic about detoxing who die extremely young, as opposed to those who work with toxic chemicals and live to an old age. I've seen people who on the surface do everything right to keep their kids as healthy as possible – organic food, no sugar, no toxins, amazing schooling and so on, yet emotionally they put their kids into terrible situations that damage their souls. They don't recognise the devastating impact of mental, emotional and energetic dysfunction as their focus is solely on the physical. From the huge amount of research I've conducted and the countless people I've tuned into, I'm clearly aware that very little of what we experience in the body is just physical.

I understand that many people have to start their inner journey by looking into the physical, changing their diet and cleansing. I believe that it is a powerful foundation to build a house on, but it is not the house. I have been inspired by stories of people who have developed their higher aspects to such a degree and have connected to incredible divine aliveness that they no longer need to eat at all and are healthy, as well as those who can eat or drink poison and have gained such control over their physical body that the toxins have very little impact on their health.

A few years ago I heard a story of a man who lived in a concentration camp during the war in the most horrifying conditions imaginable. He ate the same pitiable diet as all the other inmates, yet unlike the others who looked like skin and bones he appeared reasonably nourished. The doctors who were investigating the situation wondered if he had only just arrived in the camp but soon found out that he was one of the earliest arrivals. They scratched their heads and concluded that maybe he didn't experience as much personal trauma as everyone else. That theory quickly dwindled when they learned that his wife and four children had been killed not long after they arrived at the camp.

They eventually got him to share his secret and discovered that this man went beyond the threshold of what normal humans can handle as he realised that the only way he could stay alive and be of service to others was to transform his hatred and anger into forgiveness and compassion.

Through his incredible act of forgiveness the higher beings were able to gift this man grace, filling him with divine nourishment, which materialised in a strengthened physical body.

This is a huge question: how do we forgive the unforgivable? and is that only possible if we can somehow see the bigger picture, that this world is temporary and is here to help us learn, grow and mature? Can we stretch ourselves to become that objective in the midst of great suffering?

I just want to emphasise that forgiveness doesn't mean that we ever say that evil deeds are okay, only that we choose not to hold on to the searing pain, anger, fear and devastation they cause. To truly forgive with your whole being is also far from easy; it requires one small step after another.

At the end of the day the only way we can truly progress is to understand that we are soul-spirit beings having short bursts of physical experiences. Do we need to do what we can to keep our physical body healthy? Yes. Is what works for one totally different from another? Yes. One person can juice and fast and become extremely healthy physically, another can do the same and become violently ill as it's the wrong thing for their body, or maybe it's the wrong time of their life and they are not ready to deal with all the emotions that this type of cleansing will rouse.

What is the lesson here? We need to understand who we are, how our energy bodies and the physical body works and learn to tune in.

You are unique – remember what harms one could be the best thing possible for another.

We do not understand our own journeys, let alone other people's. To do that, we would have to be totally objective and see every detail of every life as well as all potential future lives a person has – assuming you are open to that possibility.

I believe it is time for as many people as possible to develop their own abilities to tune in and discern through a deeper understanding of self. This allows each one to follow a path that works for them no matter what anyone else thinks or believes.

✦ Transformational steps ✦

Contemplate: what aspects of yourself have you developed that are beyond the physical? What aspects of your personality would you like to refine further? This could be patience, kindness, warm-heartedness, confidence, a stronger sense of self, and so on.

Become aware of the feelings that hold you back. Are you still holding on to hurt, resentment, anger, unforgiveness? How do these emotions impact your life and health?

Is there a person or a situation that you need to forgive? It could even be yourself. Make a decision to embark on a journey of forgiveness. Go to the last section of this book and do the forgiveness process. (I suggest that you work with this process for a substantial amount of time until you feel that you have truly gained the wisdom from the difficult situation that occurred.)

The three worlds

To be whole and healthy it helps to understand our true nature in a threefold way. We human beings are the citizens of three worlds. In our body, we belong to and perceive the outer world; in our soul, we build our own inner world; and in spirit, a world that is higher than the other two reveals itself to us.

The soul is as different from spirit as it is from the body. If we simply speak of particles of carbon, oxygen and nitrogen moving around, we only have the physical body in view.

The life of the soul expresses itself through passions, desires, feelings and sensations, for instance when we taste something sweet, feel pleasure or pain, or engage in our likes or dislikes, and so on.

In the same way we do not meet our spirit if we only focus on our inner experiences and the body. The life of the spirit begins to awaken when human beings place their attention on the development of deep, objective thinking. No feeling and no enthusiasm on earth can compare with the sensations of warmth and beauty that can arise with crystal clear thoughts relating to higher worlds.

There are deeper, more objective truths which go beyond our likes and dislikes. The more we imbue ourselves with those kinds of truths, beauty and goodness the more we spiritualise our inner nature and awaken the higher members of our soul and spirit.

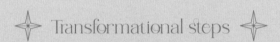

✦ Transformational steps ✦

Take some time to contemplate the idea of body, soul and spirit.

Allow yourself to tune into the possibility of connecting to higher beings and higher truths. How does it feel to sense that we are not alone? I encourage you to take some time to journal this. Also find books, teachers and other people who you can learn from or discuss your ideas with.

I encourage you to practice more objectively on a daily basis. For example, think of a person or situation and reflect how many new points of view you can find that can help you to gain a deeper understanding of what has occurred or why a particular person has acted in the way they did.

YOUR SUBTLE
BODIES

Why we need to learn about the astral body

The astral body or the star body is where you feel your pain and pleasure, your passions, desires, wishes and virtually all sensations.

The astral body needs a nervous system to incarnate into. Plants do not have a nervous system but animals do, thus they have an astral body and astral thinking.

The feelings, thoughts and will impulses you experience in the astral body will create the colours and formations of your aura. A person who has refined their intuitive abilities can look at your aura and instantly perceive your most intimate thoughts and feelings.

This subtle body extends beyond the physical body attaining impressions from all directions. It constitutes a big part of what is called a soul, but most importantly it carries your karma from one life into another.

This karma, which lives in your astral body, draws you towards challenges, opportunities, significant events, places, addictions, illnesses, health, relationships, life experiences, talents and abilities, and the purpose you have to work with in a lifetime.

How can you determine that there could be truth in this? Look at all the big events in your life.

If you tried to plan them out one by one and materialise them, would it be possible?

Look at all the little things that had to happen for you to meet some of the most important people in your life who have impacted your choices and who you are.

Think about the forces of destiny working in your astral body, leading you unconsciously towards these life experiences.

I have loved Europe since I was a child. It literally felt more like home to me than Belarus, where I was born. When I was in my mid-twenties I was lying on a couch meditating when I felt an unusual presence. Within moments I felt like an invisible being pushed me off the couch and as I was rolling on the floor, I heard the words 'you have to go and teach in Paris.' At that point I had never considered going to France. Within a few weeks I had a phone call from a lady who was living in a small holiday place in NSW that I had recently visited. At the end of the phone call she told me she was French.

Not long after she attended a workshop I was teaching. At the end of the workshop she told me she was truly impressed with what she had learned. The next time we met at an advanced workshop I was teaching, she took me aside and asked if I was interested in coming to teach in France. I knew it was destiny and six months later I was teaching in Paris which opened my heart and mind, allowed me to have the most extraordinary experiences and gave me an opportunity to travel all over Europe and many parts of the world.

The more in-tune we are with our soul, the more messages we can hear to allow us to follow our true destiny.

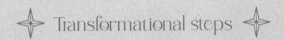

Transformational steps

Think about all the important events and people you have met in your life. Could you have consciously made that happen?

Focus on feeling connected to the universal intelligence as well as your own higher self that guides you towards your destiny.

Before going to sleep ask to be shown the next step you need to take. When you wake up journal any insights that come to you. Then courageously take a step that feels in alignment with your destiny.

Your greatest pharmacist

To truly transform we have to go beyond the way of thinking that all we have is a physical body. This can be a challenge when most of us have been conditioned to only believe in what we can see, touch and prove with scientific equipment.

Many people say that it's your brain or nervous system that is the greatest pharmacist. While it can be helpful to think that, it's not completely true. It's your astral body that is the greatest pharmacist and an inner transformer if combined with the power of your 'I am' and divine intelligence.

On the other hand, when an astral body is let loose, your life becomes full of non-stop wants, desires and sensations. The astral body can be insatiable, always wanting more of everything yet keeping your soul hollow.

It is only when your I, which is one of your higher spiritual members, makes a decision to change how you think, how you feel and how you act, that the really lasting transformation occurs not just in your health but in your soul.

Let us dive deeper into the exploration of the true role of your astral body and examine the question of why some people seem to get ill from being outside in the cold and others eat whatever they want, experience immense trauma and are under constant stress yet they hardly get sick?

Some people can argue that it is genetic. This can be a simplistic explanation; however, what if the people in your family always get ill and you don't? Or it could be the other way around, no one in your family gets sick but you do. If you want to delve deeper, a question arises: why are these particular people your parents? Why were you born in a specific country and city?

If there was no such thing as a soul and karma, wouldn't we all be equal and have the same life experiences with the same strong genes?

If we open our minds to the possibility that maybe we brought an illness or even a particularly challenging character trait from other past lives as an opportunity to learn from previous experiences, this illness could give us the greatest chance to refine and do good.

So how do we know that we might have to recompense a past deed? Because similar types of challenges are constantly pursuing us, asking us to delve deeper.

I know this is not an easy concept to digest, but it is one that strengthens you and allows you to think with immense foresight. In other words, 'I can't change what I did in the past, but I can certainly have a major influence on what happens to me and my well-being in the present and the future, thus how I act now matters!'

While not all illnesses are the result of past actions, as many of us tend to be professionals at creating dramas in our present existence, the ones that are the most difficult to overcome are likely to be karmic.

If we only think of things as physical then when the pain releases and the issue disappears we are likely to stop learning about ourselves and giving ourselves an opportunity to grow. When we begin to understand the astral body we then thank the illness for assisting us to start our healing journey and continue transforming in a way that is truly lasting.

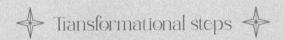

✦ Transformational steps ✦

Write down any physical conditions you may be struggling with. Ask yourself: what could be a lesson that this ailment is trying to teach me? If you don't know, you may like to check out my book, *The Secret Language of Your Body*.

Have you looked into gaining emotional wisdom from your ailments? In other words, have you worked on your fear, anger, rejection, shame, self-hate, grief and loss? If not, it may be time to start. At the end of this book I have included a process on trauma release – I encourage you to work with it in order to release any dense emotions.

Why we have to work on our energy bodies to be well

If your astral body, which contains within it your emotional body, your sensations, desires, passions, likes and dislikes becomes lazy or chaotic, it will no longer accomplish important things correctly, for instance, sorting out which food substances need to go where in your body.

If your astral body becomes clumsy and disorderly, it may not, for example, send the right substance to the heart. This in turn will greatly weaken the heart as it hasn't taken in the sufficient nourishment and instead has received an ailing substance. This unhealthy substance, which we will call refuse, then gets deposited somewhere else in your body.

As the human body is made up of a high percentage of water, this ailing refuse dissolves in the fluid. This fluid, which is now contaminated, moves through the body and affects any parts which are weak and damages those which have previously been strong. As this refuse continues to circulate, it returns to the heart, weakening it over and over again until it becomes diseased.

This is why it's vital to understand your astral body. To work with the astral body means you have to start to think about what is healthy and unhealthy for you and make courageous decisions. For instance, at this point in your life certain environments, people and activities could be detrimental to you. In order to create more peace in your nervous system you may need to move, let go of specific people and stop doing things that are harming you. This could include spending too long on social media, reading disturbing information, watching things on TV or online which numb and weaken you.

It may also involve contemplating what you spend most of your time thinking about and how those thoughts affect you. You might be required to change your perspective on how you live your life and start to consciously monitor your thoughts and feelings.

Art therapy, meditation, a movement practice, gardening, loving thoughts and feelings, knowing your purpose and learning how to become a more balanced person in your outer and inner life can greatly help you to refine your astral body.

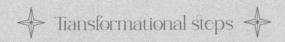

✦ Transformational Steps ✦

What or whom are you willing to let go of to become healthier?

What emotions are you ready to release?

What creative activity are you willing to embrace in order to start re-nourishing yourself?

I also encourage you to work with the process for healing your body at the end of this book as well as working with your shadow.

Your etheric body

The etheric body or life body is related to the plant kingdom. This subtle body gives form to the physical body, as without it, the different parts of the physical body would fall apart.

A part of our etheric body comes from our parents and carries hereditary forces within it. The same cosmic and earthly forces which enable the plants to grow also give us our growth; this is etheric energy or prana.

To an intuitive or a clairvoyant, the etheric body looks like a copy of the physical body with all its bones, muscles and organs. Before any illness appears in the physical body, it will impact the etheric body first.

The etheric body permeates the physical in all its parts and can be seen as its architect.

So often we complain and wonder why we are not creating the type of experiences we desire; however, if we had extra sensory vision and could see what our limiting, fearful thoughts which have been fed and fed and fed over many years look like, we would not be surprised.

Our etheric body, which is a life body as well as a body of memory and habit, stores these thought forms. Eventually these heavy, limiting, every-day-is-the-same, survival, fear, hurt and trauma-based thoughts create a hardening of the etheric body.

When the etheric body is hardened enough, your ability to stretch, grow, learn, heal and evolve greatly diminishes. As you rebuild a fortress out of this new hardened etheric substance around you, life becomes heavier and darker and no matter which way you look, you only see pain, fear, limitation and lack. And of course, sickness!

When you become conscious, you start to invest your time, effort and energy into a new type of thinking and living.

You start to be aware of the things that harden your etheric body, for instance, spending too much time interacting with technology, watching TV, drinking alcohol, being harsh and critical, focusing on lack, taking any type of synthetic or recreational drugs, lack of love, intimacy and nurturing.

You also realise that your old, outdated thinking has now become a big part of your habits, which means it's going to take time, effort and persistence to change.

The things that soften your etheric body are art, beauty, creativity, movement, love, heart openness, deep and profound thinking, and an interest and understanding of the divine forces.

As your etheric body strengthens you start to think in a more creative way, your energy revitalises and your health dramatically improves.

✦ Transformational steps ✦

I encourage you to find some quiet time, grab a journal and explore what thoughts you are thinking over and over again. How do they serve you or limit you?

What old patterns are you ready to face and let go of? Are you willing to explore the feelings that are attached to them? What experiences are these feelings connected to? Can you find anything you can learn from those experiences, that can move you forward?

I also encourage you to work with the ancestral release process in the back section of this book.

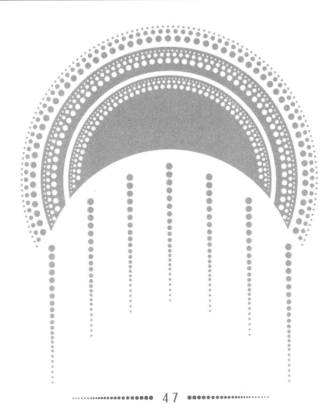

Ego

Our I or ego relates us to the human kingdom; it is what makes us individuals; there is no other I exactly like you. The animals don't have an individual ego; they have a group ego working down upon them from the astral world.

The magical word I is the wonderful high-level word of soul, which makes us independent beings. You can only be an I to yourself; the other is a you.

In this very small word lies great depths of possibility for the evolution of our soul.

With a strong sense of I we become the masters of our selves and our lower impulses. The ego or I can use thinking to penetrate into the lower bodies and spiritualise them.

The ego in the hidden mystery circles has been portrayed as having the quality of the double-edged sword. One side is the hardening egotist (this is when the astral body hardens the I and engulfs it.) Egotists only care about their own comfort and desires and mostly focus on having material possessions and getting what they want no matter the impact. They want to own the biggest house on the biggest piece of land, have the most expensive and beautiful clothes, furniture, cars, yachts, planes and party it up, with little care that a huge part of the world live in poverty, struggle and are in constant pain. They also don't care who they use or hurt in their pursuit of pleasure and comfort.

The other side of the sword is the softening into our inner journey which awakens the divine drop of the Godhead that we each have within us – our higher self.

We can use our I to awaken our spirit and continue to progress on our journey of evolution, or we can allow our desire for luxuries, comfort and indolence to stifle it.

The stronger our I is, the more capable we become of the highest levels of transformation, healing and awakening.

 Transformational steps

What have you been putting off for some time that would be healthy for you to do? Is it meditation, doing self-healing processes, a movement practice?

Make a commitment to put between five and 30 mins a day 3-5 days a week towards what would be healthy for your own inner growth and awakening. The more you follow through on those commitments the better you will feel about yourself, and new and empowering possibilities will open up to you. You will also find yourself standing strong in what you believe and in turn inspire greater trust from others.

I encourage you to do the strengthening your I am process at the end of this book and observe how much more empowered you feel.

CELESTIAL BEINGS AND
A COSMIC EXPLORATION

Why comfort can lead to stagnation

While most of us are taught to strive for comfort our whole lives, when we actually examine the times we have felt comfortable as opposed to challenged, we can easily determine that comfort leads to complacency, boredom and stagnation. You can see that clearly in every area of life.

If your physical health is good then you have no incentive to learn about how to eat healthy, look after your body or understand the impact your thoughts and feelings have on your health. Thus, in your comfort you are likely to mistreat your body until it eventually becomes ill.

In our intimate relationships, most of us desire a profound connection, understanding, sensitivity, love and a feeling of belonging. Many of us start from a place of neediness and some sense of brokenness, giving to each other what we have been missing and searching for. However, that phase can only last so long. After a few years many people become comfortable in their relationships, even if there are major challenges and aspects of the relationship where they are not connecting, listening, understanding or supporting each other. They become comfortable in what they know, yet lack of growth creates stagnation and a profound inner dissatisfaction. So of course, as time goes on, if we don't put in the deep work, we notice less loving warmth and more coldness in our intimate life with another.

Rather than two individuals who are constantly growing, evolving, refining and inspiring each other, we stay together because it's easier, we have kids, we don't want to be alone, we don't know how to make money, and so on. And more than anything we are terrified to let go of our comfort and open ourselves to something new. People then wonder why there are so many who are being unfaithful or why there is so much divorce.

Profound trust in any relationship awakens when you are willing to go beyond comfort and open your heart and soul to another, showing them all your broken bits and then taking full responsibility for yourself and your willingness to transform as opposed to wallowing in your misfortune. Most of us are both afraid and desperate to witness growth in each other, which can awaken deeper layers of love, understanding and appreciation, yet we are not taught to value our connections with others.

What we are taught to value is money, recognition, success and most of all comfort – and of course in comfort we usually take things for granted. All these things in themselves can be very helpful, as long as one is also willing to continually evolve.

Think about your career – if you have to do the same thing over and over again with nothing new that challenges or inspires you, eventually your inner being will become tense, hardened and complacent and you will end up spending much of your time complaining.

Our soul can grow through wisdom, compassion and love as well as through trials and tribulations.

We need to ask ourselves: which part of our soul is attracted only to pleasure and comfort? From my exploration, it comes from our lower, astral, materialistic nature.

When you truly understand the cycle of incarnation, you realise that ill fortune needs to be met with the same sense of appreciation as one would meet good fortune. Because so-called ill fortune, if seen correctly, could be leading you to good fortune.

If I want to avoid things that hurt me then I'm unknowingly saying to myself, I'm okay with my weaknesses and imperfections. Whereas every time I meet a challenge and an obstacle and I grow in humility, forgiveness and selfless love, then I've overcome an old weakness of mine.

So, every day, month and year I get to work on deeper aspects of my soul, evolving to higher possibilities as opposed to having to repeat the same old painful lessons.

When you truly think into the possibility of evolution, it changes your soul and how you are inspired to live.

A new point of view could be to be open to and accepting of discomfort, as it's what offers us the deepest opportunity to grow, and also be grateful for when you are comfortable, knowing that both are temporary.

This is not an easy teaching but it's the one that, if truly grasped, can lead to much expansion, a polishing of our inner diamond and a revelation of higher wisdom.

Transformational steps

What aspect of your life have you put into the too-hard basket?

How does this shadow part limit you from being all of you and thus hold you back?

How willing are you to embrace all of you in order to fully live your soul's destiny?

I encourage you to do the shadow process at the end of this book for at least a month in order to embrace more of who you truly are.

General vs specific in naming the divine

I t seems like we have many names for the divine forces that we experience. What I'd like to explore is how we can be less general in referring everything to the universe and learn to become a little more specific.

One day I sat and thought, 'When I say the universe will give me this or that, what am I actually saying? And by being so completely general am I referring to the powers of benevolence or darkness?' As when I ask for something from the universe I need to understand that both light and dark beings live here!

It's like having someone who has never seen a person before look at a human who has a head, arms, legs, chest, back, hips, legs and so on and point at the different parts of the body with a question of what is that? To be told, 'It's part of the universal human.'

When there are no distinctions and everything is being perceived as the universal person, we have no understanding of any part of an individual or any point of reference of which parts could be ailing and need more attention.

When we clump everything together into the universe, we oversimplify the whole spiritual existence and thus cheat ourselves out of a more accurate higher truth or understanding of life in spiritual realms.

How many people really think about what is meant by the many mystical words that get thrown around with very little thought for what they are? We are beginning to recognise more and more that our thoughts and words have the power to strengthen us or to make us bedridden in the throes of the deepest pain and darkness.

After much resistance I started to dedicate more time and effort to learning about higher truths, and through that study I discovered that there is really no such thing as a generalised energy for the universe.

When we only focus on oversimplifying everything, we truly live on the surface and are ruled both by generalisations and also by many of our so-called unconscious impulses.

Every city and every country has a particular etheric sphere that you either feel a sympathy with or an antipathy. In other words, you either feel at home in a place and add loving peaceful energy to it or you feel uncomfortable or even repulsed and create more suffering and conflict there.

Moreover, there are also very conscious archangelic beings who create a unique field of expression in each country and city with all its colourful particulars. And of course, there are also beings of darkness which dwell in each city, especially around the areas where there have been violent outbursts, wars, hatred, aggression, abuse, sickness, egotism, greed, focus on money, power and death. Think of all the atrocities human beings have been capable of. You know clearly that we have not only been influenced by the powers of light.

Each heavenly being from an angel to a throne to the beings who wear dark hats are as unique as each human is.

What I have come to understand from tuning in to people for 20 years and in my constant desire for clarification is that there are very conscious beings operating in areas of our soul we call the unconscious, it's just that we are not consciously aware of them. However, we all know that we don't usually purposefully sabotage the things that we have yearned for, for many years. We don't consciously say, I need to be sick to learn a lesson, we also don't fully understand the anger, anxiety, fear or depression that takes over us and how exactly this has occurred and why. Yet we feel it when we are taken over by a variety of unpleasant and also pleasant feelings. So, what is really going on in our so-called unconscious?

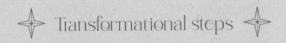

✦ Transformational steps ✦

There is so much we don't understand. However, I believe that we are living in a time where our souls are developed enough to not only desire to understand but need to understand the divine.

Thus instead of generalising, the opportunity is to become curious and to learn. You can start by asking yourself: when I say universe, who am I really referring to? What am I asking for? Am I asking for something connected to myself, in which case a high likelihood is that I'm going to be connecting to my angel or am I asking for someone that can help me with my relationships in which case an archangel could be involved? Before going to sleep, focus on your guardian angel; ask this being to guide you towards whatever is the next step for your highest good in divine order and divine timing. If you are having issues in a relationship, call on an archangel who can help you to understand each other from your heart and soul. When you wake up, have a journal next to your bed and write down any insights. Take time to sit with those and then take action.

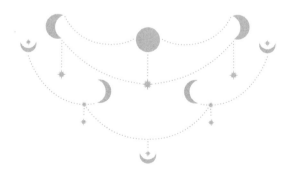

Angels and their role

While I have always believed in angels and higher heavenly beings, I have never resonated with fluffy feel-good explanations that essentially say angels are genies to make your every wish come true, all you have to do is ask.

What I have explored is the different roles that angels, archangels, archai and even higher heavenly beings perform for humanity.

A lot of these experiences occurred when I was having a difficult time but were so impactful that I had to take notice. Later I was extremely fortunate to find some truly evolved teachers to help me to consciously understand who these beings are.

I have discovered that at some point when we open our hearts and minds enough we will experience an impulse from the angelic realm to want to understand the deeper nature of the human being including our true make-up, where we came from, how we were created and where we are going.

We will then meet every person and every experience with the profound understanding that the divine essence is at work in everyone and everything. It will no longer be just a thought but an enlivening experience. Every encounter we undergo with another will then become sacred.

As we understand more and more about the difference between the soul, spirit and the role of our I, we will develop a stronger ability to raise our consciousness and bring a true understanding of the spiritual world and our role in it into our lives.

To gain an intimate relationship with our angel we need to develop a love for all the beings we encounter in the physical as well as spiritual worlds, therefore our thoughts and feelings need to be of a higher nature.

More and more we need to experience awe for the world above us that we can't see but which permeates ours.

As we become aware of our deeper self new sensitivities arise. We begin to feel beyond doubt that we undergo multiple earth lives and realise that we have an angel who guides, leads and directs each one of us. Our angels hold our higher self and our karma from all our past lives until we are consciously ready to work with our destiny.

In each of our incarnations angels create images inside our astral body for us to understand their intentions. This is why when we become sensitive and tune in, we can experience immense insight and guidance. This can also at times occur during traumatic experiences.

When I was 19 years old I got pregnant. It was a very difficult experience for me and something I wasn't quite ready for. After much reflection I decided to have the baby. At around 37 weeks I had a strong feeling that something was wrong with the baby's heart. I spoke to the midwife about it and she told me that everything was okay and I needed to focus on being positive and it was alright if the baby didn't move much. I felt a bit reassured but was still very uncomfortable. A week later I went into labour. My then husband drove me to the hospital. When I got in, someone put their hand on my belly and asked me when was the last time that I felt the baby move. I had a contraction and didn't know how to answer.

Not long after this I gave birth. When the baby came out it was silent in the room. I asked if everything was okay. The nurse told me, 'I'm sorry.' I went into total shock. In my mind I was thinking, 'What is wrong with me?' Not long after as I was staring at the ceiling I saw an angel. The moment I saw it I felt calm. The angel was holding two children. It told me not to worry and that I would have two children soon. It then disappeared. I felt strengthened, inspired and in awe. For the next several hours I knew that somehow the death of this baby, as hard as it was, would change my life and lead me to discover more of my soul journey in order to learn about the spiritual world. I also had hope that I would have two children.

Seven months later I got pregnant and had my son. Just over two years after that I had my daughter. My experience with my angel gave me the impetus to explore and the courage to try again.

The angel's impulses for us are universal love which is a total shift in our social behaviour.

On the highest level this means no human could be truly happy while other people suffer on earth without trying to do something to help them.

Our angels also strive to grant us the ability to see each other's auras, which allow us to let go of a sense of separation and judgements based on where we were born, the colour of our skin, the religion we believe in and the amount of material possessions we have on loan (as none of us get to take them with us when we pass the threshold.)

In the future every meeting of two humans will reveal what is in their soul and spirit through their auras. People will have developed their intuitive capacities to such a degree that when they meet, they will be able to see each other's auras. Each person's aura will reveal what they really think, feel and hold dear. Therefore, it will become easier to decipher who is coming from a place of goodness, benevolence and selflessness and who is carrying malice, selfishness and a hunger for power within their being.

Our angels are constantly trying to enable each of us to reach the wisdom of the spirit through our ability for profound thinking.

Our angel is raised to lofty heights if we think thoughts of higher worlds and embrace loving, honourable ideals. In the same spiritual principal, our angel is dragged down below if we only think selfish, material thoughts of everyday physical existence. While our angel never abandons us, if we become too materialistic we may not be able to perceive it or communicate with it, neither here and potentially even after we cross over.

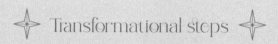

✦ Transformational steps ✦

You are able to communicate with your angel daily by asking yourself: what can I do today in order to become the best version of myself? Then give yourself a moment of quiet time to truly hear this message.

You can also work on letting go of judgements about others and trying to see what is good, holy and beautiful in them.

On a practical level, you can attempt to help and support anyone who needs your assistance.

Archangels and their role

Most of us have heard about archangels; however, there has been a lot of confusing and conflicting information circulating. Below are some of the discoveries I have made through my research which have resonated in my soul.

Archangels are also called spirits of fire. Once you have reached the capacity to perceive your angel in what's called creative imagination, then through expanded love and devotion you can go beyond the self and start focusing on what is happening in the world. In the same way that you have your guide through your angel, there are also nations and tribes who belong together and are being guided by the archangels. These archangels also guide our angels.

It's important to understand that if two or more people come together an archangel appears. Thus, whenever you spend time with someone else you are not only dealing with them, but also their angel and an archangel who is interwoven into the feelings between the two of you in your relationship.

Archangels also help to guide and develop different languages, allowing the people of all the nations to express themselves in a variety of ways.

This is why each country has such a unique feeling. I remember one of my first visits to Paris. I was standing next to a monument of an angel when my heart opened and I felt the city of Paris connected to me and it poured aliveness into my heart. When I tuned into my heart I saw an image of a tree that had been dying from thirst and was finally receiving the life force it needed. This was my first taste of love, creativity and adventure which awaited me in that city.

We can also connect with the archangels by speaking of spiritual ideals, understanding the process between death and rebirth and developing an inner enthusiasm for higher spiritual knowledge.

Most of our interactions with the angels and archangels happen during sleep within our astral body which is why it is so important to live your day correctly and prepare for sleep. When your connection with the archangels is deep, you wake up feeling alive, full of vigour and with the capacity to handle whatever comes your way.

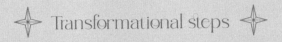

Transformational steps

Below is a powerful meditation based off Rudolf Steiner's that I have practised for years to strengthen myself and connect to the angelic realm.

It is best to do this standing up.

Say: steadfastly, I take my place on earth. Take a small step forward with your left leg. Feel the energy circulating, connecting you to your deeper self.

Take a small step forward with your right leg and say: with certainty I walk the path of life. Feel the energy circulating in your left leg.

Then feel the streams from both legs move into the heart and say: strength pours into my heart. Feel as immense strength from the angelic realm pours into your heart.

Feel as the energy in your heart becomes warm. Say: love at the core of my being. Open your left arm and let the warmth flow down your arm and out of your palms.

Then open your right arm, say: hope in everything I do. Feel as the energy moves down your right arm into the palms of your hands.

Radiate hope from the palms of your hands.

Now let all the energy you have generated move up into your head. Allow the light from your head to connect to your angel, archangel, archai and higher beings. Then feel as their wisdom is being poured down into your crown and down through your whole body into your feet. Say: trust in all my thinking.

I encourage you to practise this meditation twice daily in particular in the morning and evening time.

Who are the archai?

I wanted to briefly introduce the archai as not many people have heard of or know much about these incredibly evolved beings. They are also known as primal beginnings or spirits of personality.

When we start to learn about the evolution of humanity we realise that whole time periods like the Egyptian cultural period, when Egypt had enormous power and the pyramids were built, or the Roman period, when Rome reigned, had a certain character to it. That character or the stamp of that period was under the leadership of a being. That being is called a time spirit or the archai.

The archai take turns at leading certain periods. In 1879 when Kali Yuga – the dark ages – ended, Archangel Michael evolved to a higher post and became the time spirit of our time and will be for the next several hundred years or so. Let's deepen our exploration of the roles these beings played.

The archai give you the strength to fully incarnate into your body and use the ego to take charge of the drives and the instincts of the body.

You only gain the strength you require to make inner freedom part of your life if you have the right relationship with the archai as you enter into sleep. The archai work with your I during sleep. Although you might be in an unconscious state, the archai are able to perceive what you did during the day and then help you develop a distinct sense of satisfaction or dissatisfaction around what occurred.

This deeply impacts your future karma and destiny.

To improve your intimacy with the archai during sleep, you have to develop a deep love for humanity without judgement. You must learn to be genuinely interested in every person that comes into your life.

Your relationship with the archai and in particular whether you were able to develop a real love for humanity does not only occur during one life. However, the stronger your relationship is the more you receive the physical strength, balance and the capacity to control your glandular function and other aspects of your physical and emotional well-being in your future incarnation.

Your mind, heart and will can only be free if you have established the right relationship to the archangels in your heart and mind and the right relationship to the archai in your will. Otherwise, your will can create major obstacles to your ability to develop independent thinking.

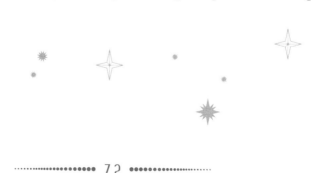

Transformational steps

The archai of our time is Michael. Michael helps us to face our limitations and our shadow and to embrace our strength and intuition. Michael also gives us courage.

Call on this being whenever you need more courage to move forward, especially in difficult times. Also please work on the shadow process and strengthening your I am process at the back of the book.

A look at the hierarchies and their roles

One of the questions many people may have asked during their lives is: are we here alone or do we have help?

And if we do have higher help, who are these beings and what is their role?

To be able to connect with these heavenly helpers, we may need to learn a little about them as well as to understand what each provides. I have explored a little in this book about the angels, as these are the closest being connected to us. In fact, each one of us has a guardian angel that guides us throughout our lives. This guardian angel holds the wisdom of our destiny and is constantly attempting to encourage us and guide us forward. Unfortunately, most of us tend to ignore the messages by numbing our spiritual senses. I have also written basic explanations about the archangels and the archai. I have mentioned the rest of the beings of the hierarches here in a very superficial way, in order to pique the interest of those who are ready to learn more, as there is so much more to learn.

If you are ready, I encourage you to explore spiritual science and the work of Rudolf Steiner. Ideally starting with his basic work on theosophy, and then moving towards other areas of interest step by step.

Below is a very simplistic outline of study about the qualities the higher beings may exude as well as the role they have played in co-creating our universe, our bodies and the opportunity for us to reside here and grow.

The angels can be viewed as messengers of the divine spiritual world. They are our closest guides.

The archangels can be seen as folk spirits and can help to guide nations. We can observe the influence of the archangels whenever we travel to different countries, with their variety of rich cultures and languages.

The archai are also known as spirits of time and take turns to lead the whole of humanity. At this point in our evolution we are being led by Archai Michael.

The archi, archangels and angels are the beings who are connected to the third hierarchy and have the closest direct influence on human beings.

The second hierarchies include exusiai, which are recognised as spirits of form. Dynamis, who are seen as spirits of motion and kyriotetes, known as the spirits of wisdom.

The first hierarchies consist of thrones – the spirits of will, cherubim – the spirits of harmony, and seraphim – the spirits of love.

It is important to understand that just as human beings are involved in the process of evolution, so are the beings of the hierarchies.

Here is a very brief, incredibly simplified description of how these celestial beings work together in a way that I have understood so far.

The possibility for our whole existence occurred when God or source inspired the highest members of the first hierarchy – the seraphim – to create free human beings and an environment where they could evolve. Through their contemplation of this mission, the seraphim used their creative forces to manifest the world into existence in a purely spiritual form. The cherubim then worked together to bring practicality and harmony to this 'spiritual world' in conjunction with other star systems in the universe. The thrones then used their will to create the initial foundation of the world and human beings.

The beings of the second hierarchy, the kyriotetes, dynamis and exusiai fashioned the solar system and began to work on the formation of the physical body.

The role of the beings of the third hierarchy, with the support of the higher hierarchies, has been to mould, refine and perfect the prototypes which would be able to accommodate the soul and the spirit of a human being. A being who would have the capacity to be independent in their thinking, feeling and will.

It is important to understand that the human experiment has been created in order to give rise to something new, something that has not existed before in the realm of the higher hierarchies.

This is freedom.

All the hierarchies, besides the human, strictly follow and adhere to the word of God. Thus, they will wear metaphoric white hats and act in a beautiful, loving, aligned way with the will of God, or they will wear so called black hats if they are given a contrary impulse, thus offering human beings choice between good and bad, right and wrong. (Of course, this is much more complex and layered than can be written in a few lines.)

A human being has an opportunity to evolve into the tenth hierarchy through all the challenges as well as highs and lows they experience in this physical world, where good and evil roam. Through the cycle of death and rebirth a human being has an opportunity to evolve into a free, unique, loving human being.

✦ Transformational steps ✦

Please meditate on what I have written in this chapter. Some of the concepts may seem a little repetitive, as I am trying to explore a particular understanding from a slightly different perspective in each segment. I also want you to be able to pick up this book and read a chapter and be reminded of the most important understandings around higher beings.

I encourage you to take some time to journal on where in your life you feel a sense of freedom of choice and where you feel controlled by other people.

Explore how it feels to be controlled and told what to do. Does this make you feel like rebelling? If so, reflect on what could be a healthy rebellion within you, as opposed to unhealthy; for example, healthy could involve study, education, learning to think for yourself, self-healing and sharing new ideas with those who are open to it. Unhealthy could involve erupting and attacking others, any type of violence, repression and censorship.

Keep moving towards freedom and healthy rebellion.

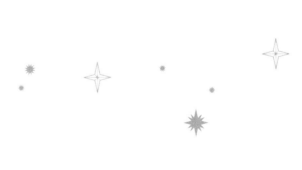

So why not simply connect to God?

This is a major discussion and obviously a very sensitive one for many people. As God has a different meaning based on where you grew up and whose point of view you took on I therefore want to approach this topic from my particular understanding with full respect that you will discover your own meaning.

For many years, I felt I had a powerful connection with God, in fact I would think, 'Why would I need to learn about or communicate to this or that being, learn about an angel, archangel, or an evolved master when I can simply connect to God and bypass all the so-called minor beings?'

However, for years I would tune into many people who talked about their direct connection with God and I would find that there was an aspect of their soul that was empty and darkened. It was like a part of their soul got stunted. I, of course, found the same in myself. It was a feeling of soul emptiness and a sense that I had a black hat on top of my head that stopped me from connecting to something higher. By the time I turned 30 I felt that I was going around and around in circles recycling old information without any significant spiritual insights that could inspire or incite me to look further.

Eventually I found some profound teachings on the nine hierarchies of heavenly beings who resided in various planets orbiting the stars. This is when astrology began to make sense to me. The first realm beyond our physical that I began to learn about in more detail was the angelic realm. I don't want to put down people's various beliefs but let's say that the information I was exposed to that rang true in my soul came from these beings who were initiated into the divine hidden mysteries, the most famous being Buddha, Moses, Zarathustra, Saint John and Rudolf Steiner.

In fact, if you look at some of the most famous artists such as Raphael, Michelangelo, Leonardo da Vinci, Lucas Cranach the Elder, Giotto and Matthias Grünewald who have also been initiated into the hidden mysteries, they have all depicted various aspects of spiritual worlds and heavenly beings so that those who desire to explore deeper can understand evolution and hidden wisdom through their paintings. (Again, I don't want to sound like there are superior and inferior people, just that there are those who choose to research and understand spiritual worlds in a particular form and those who focus their attention more on the present moment and the importance of the physical world. Both are valid and important to explore.)

I personally realised that you can't demand to go to university if you haven't even finished grade one. You can't learn about algebra if you don't even know how to do multiplication and division, and it's unlikely that you can jump straight into communicating with

God when you have not understood any of the angelic beings who have greatly contributed to you having a physical, etheric and astral body as well as the development of your soul and spirit. Most of whose efforts we are totally unaware of. Yet we are all being called to wake up and understand more about our true nature.

My years of research and tuning in led me to believe that the closest spiritual being to us is our angel. This angel comes with us into every life and holds our karma and our destiny. Depending on how we live, we either uplift our angel or we take this heavenly being into darkness, or even sub-nature.

I know this is going to be a big statement, and as I have previously said I do not make it lightly, I believe that what many people call God is actually their angel. Logically it makes sense that in order to experience and know God, you may need to understand the nine hierarchies of spiritual beings, as well as Christ and the Holy Spirit which lead up to God. The same way that primary school leads to high school and high school leads to university.

When mentioning Christ, I am aware that people have a variety of beliefs about this heavenly being. I am not referring to various Christian religious teachings. I am referring to my years of study of Christ, an exalted being, who came into the physical world to help us evolve. This heavenly being has also been instrumental in helping us develop our sense of morality and integrity as well as awakening our individuality and ability to think for ourselves and to embody the wisdom of the Ten Commandments.

So as many people (I was one of them) think of their angel as God and it's far from the truth as they don't understand who God or an angel really is, they create confusion in their soul. Confusion leads to deadness and becoming stuck on a spiritual level. When we stagnate spiritually it impacts our ability to think, stretch, expand, feel, be well and evolve. The more we are stuck the more we can lose ourselves and our individuality and start to follow beliefs, ideas and ways for living that do not serve us and potentially lead us into materialism and self-focus.

Thus spiritual lies or half-truths (of which there are many) can cause a major destruction of our inner being. We have to start thinking about these things in a logical, connected way and be willing to research and invest time into these aspects which are eternal as opposed to only the limited aspects of survival that we usually focus on.

I am not saying that you don't have a relationship with God or that you don't have a drop of the divine essence within you. What I am saying is that your understanding and connection with God or Christ could deepen profoundly if you understood all the beings who were involved in you having the physical, etheric, astral and ego bodies. From my experience when you do, God takes on a very profound meaning and this opens your heart in awe.

Many people talk about the father God and the son God. From what I have learned the father God impacts what is predetermined, stable, has already been formed and is meant to happen. The father is connected to all of life and in particular influences what we need to experience in order to learn and grow. This can also be understood as our destiny.

The son God, who is known as Christ, offers us our freedom and a possibility to choose something new and different in order to grow, evolve and awaken our unexplored and unforeseen creative faculties. In doing so, Christ offers us the potential of creating something new in the future that may not have yet been produced.

As we learn, grow and discover new aspects of life and ourselves, it impacts all the heavenly beings including Christ and God.

From my limited understanding, God had an impulse to create a free human race, which from their own inner calling and freedom of choice would want to connect to love and to God, even if this human being was tempted into darkness. The higher beings who wear the white hats and do good, as well as those who wear dark hats and bring pain and challenge, are still following the orders of God, while we are at the forefront of choice and free will. We can choose to come from a space of love and goodness or from evil and harm.

Of course this can open the door to profound discussions from many perspectives.

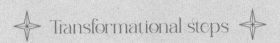

Transformational steps

This has been my personal exploration and understanding. I encourage you to open your mind and make time to do your own research and in doing so develop your own wisdom.

If my exploration has inspired you, do some research about angelic realms. My personal suggestion is to look into Esoteric Christian writings. I have found Rudolf Steiner's work particularly impactful. However, his work requires immense patience, both with the language as well as the difficulty of the material.

If you connect to a particular culture or if you were born into a certain religion you may like to explore there. Esoteric knowledge refers to a hidden or even lost wisdom. There are also incredible insights that we can receive from indigenous knowledge. Start where you feel the most comfortable and keep checking with yourself by asking: does this resonate within my soul?

The past and the future – the moon and the sun forces

From my research and understanding, clarity and discernment of what most call the universe helps us to enrich our souls. So, from both intuitively being able to see into the body and reflecting on what is meant by the many generalised terms we use, I believe that there are highly evolved as well as highly destructive beings that impact our lives.

If we just call everything energy then we deaden our capacity to discern who it is that has this energy. A great question to ask is: is the energy dead or alive? If we consider that this energy could be alive, then we also have to ask if it actually comes from living beings.

I like to think into things from a logical perspective, therefore let's explore the moon and the sun.

Most people can feel the impact of the moon and its forces, especially as we enter into the time of the full moon. We can also feel the power of the sun and how it physically influences us when it warms our bodies, yet very few people understand much about the beings who live on the moon and on the sun. They may not have the same physical bodies as us, but they certainly impact our feelings and our destiny.

From my studies, I have discovered that the moon connects us to the past. It also links us with our abiding necessity. In other words, whatever we need to experience here on earth – this could be meeting particular people, for instance family members, being born into a certain environment and country, the talents and abilities that awaken within us, the people we meet who change our lives, specific events that take us into a new direction – our karmic destiny is connected to the forces and the heavenly beings of the moon. Therefore when you meet someone and it's a moon meeting, you are likely to either feel a deep love or a deep dislike towards them. Either way, there is a familiarity. You are also likely to constantly think about them and even have them visit your dreams.

The sun and its heavenly hosts connect us to everything that offers us the possibilities of freedom and the future. When it's a sun meeting, it feels fresh, new and full of opportunities. That meeting can last a few minutes or it can be a new experience that you are co-creating for the rest of your life. This encounter feels lighter, freer and has a sense of ease to it.

I was relieved to hear a very wise teacher once share that rather than entering into deep intimate relationships with those we have heavy baggage with, we should really look for partners with whom we can create fresh possibilities.

However, let's go into a deeper exploration of the moon experience; for example, you might have been born in a particular country yet have a destiny to meet someone on the other side of the world. I was born in Belarus but I couldn't stay there, as it was vital my family move to Australia. In fact, my mum was told that if she chose to stay in Belarus and do nothing, my brother would die. He was the impetus my mother needed to take action.

It is important to understand that everyone in your family is connected to your karma and destiny.

Just take a moment to think about an experience you had to have to grow or a person you had to meet who changed your life. Then reflect on your life. One different turn of events and you may not have ever met this person or had a particular experience.

Could you really be that smart as to plan out all these events without divine help? Obviously not all of our experiences with other people are pleasant. Some are extremely difficult, yet they are the ones that make us review, transform and take massive steps forward. The more we connect with our inner selves and understand some deeper truths, the more we can welcome as opposed to fight those experiences that gave us our greatest opportunity to grow.

I'm sharing all this because when we start to develop some understanding of how the sun and the moon influence us, we can start to awaken the awe for the higher beings who both guide and offer us the freedom to grow. We need to learn how to think in more specific ways, rather than generalise everything as the universe. At the same time we need to be aware that as much as there are many holy beings, there are also dark entities who tempt us to be dishonourable, dishonest, selfish and to take advantage of others. As we become more conscious we start to differentiate between the various beings and how they impact our lives. The more we understand their role and learn about ourselves, the more autonomous we become.

Transformational steps

Journal on some of your most difficult experiences with others and how they made you grow, then write down your most joyful experiences with others and how those have made you grow.

Take some time to contemplate what is working in your life and what you are ready to let go of.

YOUR SOUL, KARMA, AND THE SPIRITUAL REALM

Have you ever really thought about how amazing it is that you can think?

In life you have the choice to think about the most menial things but also the most advanced things. I've always been curious and asked deep questions about how things really work. For example, how does daylight and night-time, winter, summer, autumn and spring occur? What happens during sleep? Where do we go when we lose consciousness and why is it that at certain times we wake up tired and at other times re-energised? What are the different things that our angel does and how does it become impacted by how we think, feel and live?

I actually heard a great teacher say: 'if you have a pet that you love, do you look after it, give it food, possibly take it for a walk, cuddle it and make sure that it's safe and loved?' He proceeded to say that maybe to your angel you are like the most beloved pet and this angel does its best to look after you. While you forget that you have had many previous lives, your angel remembers and tries to send images into your astral body to help you with what you may experience as intuitive insights to connect with this or that person, do this or that thing, find a particular book or teaching and so on, in order to follow the path that you, with the assistance of higher, heavenly beings, have designed.

From my research and understanding, I believe your angel provides the energy, the space and the substance of thought; however, what we think about at every moment comes from our individual self. Therefore, the question arises: 'how does what I think about affect my angel? Do my thoughts take it to higher states of consciousness and bring it joy or does my self-involvement and certain actions drag my angel down?'

Imagine if we all started to exercise the kind of thinking that went beyond our temporary issues and what we want and into the kind of thinking and feeling about the most important deeds that would assist those around us?

What would be helpful to our partner, our child, our friend and our angel?

What if we also realised that our thought substance was actually alive? Would we be more conscious and responsible of what thoughts we entertain?

Would we begin to desire to entertain, explore and feed higher thoughts that had to do with a much more interesting and evolved thinking, for example the evolution of humanity and all the heavenly beings which are involved?

Would we think about ourselves more as a soul and spirit being and wonder what our soul needs in order to grow? Would we go further and ask: What kind of things awaken my spirit? What kind of truths are there which are based on things we don't know but would like to discover?

When you contemplate those big topics would you be truly satisfied with instant one-line answers or would you want the richness of a daily discovery of more profound wisdom, the kind of wisdom that required you to use your thinking to create connections and from those connections grow new branches, new leaves and flowers?

If you knew there was no end to your discovery, would you become overwhelmed and want to stop learning, or become joyously enthusiastic that you could always discover more depth and that when the time came to let go of your borrowed physical body you would come back to your spiritual home full of immense wealth of eternal wisdom? The kind of wisdom that would open the doors to creative bliss of the higher worlds.

While it can be very attractive to an aspect of you to have fast, instant, easy and effortless answers and experiences, this does not always lead you to the profundity and the awakening of truth, beauty and goodness of your inner life that takes time, a strong foundation and deep transformation that your soul desires.

✦ Transformational steps ✦

Become aware of what kind of thoughts you are nourishing and whether they are lifting you and your angel up or if they are creating a sense of deadness and frustration.

For the next seven days, consciously focus on uplifting thoughts and deeds. In fact, stretch yourself and do something surprisingly positive for someone who doesn't expect it.

Why do we need to learn about spiritual worlds while we are on earth?

The main way we can learn about what happens in the spiritual worlds and where we spend a huge amount of our time is through studying this topic on earth. Without having any understanding of what happens in the higher worlds, we might spend a protracted period of time being attached to the things in the material world which create more fear, karma and pain.

Think about it. You are unlikely to go to a country you have never been to without learning something about that nation: its geography, what to do there, what precautions you may need to take, where to visit, where to stay and what language or languages they speak. So why do people think they don't need to learn anything about the spiritual spheres until they pass over?

It's only through understanding and preparation that we can give ourselves a possibility to have a conscious, empowered, invigorated journey in the spirit realm, as opposed to an oblivious, uncomfortable and weakened experience.

If your passage through the spiritual realms is conscious, then you are more likely to receive inner strength, gifts, wisdom and an ability to go through your next life with a lot more potency, deepening all your capacities for profound thinking, understanding, love, healing, leadership, artistic talents, extensive super-sensible abilities, beneficial discoveries, strengthened values and continuous evolution. Rather than working on basic survival and struggles, you will have much more intricate, heartfelt and interesting interactions and life experiences.

When you understand what really occurs during different phases of your life after death, you are likely to make profound changes to how you live your life and the things you place value on. This is going to positively influence many aspects of your future life, including the kind of body you are likely to receive, what kind of parents you will have and which part of the world you will be born into, as well as the types of talents and abilities you will be able to express.

Your capacity to deal with challenges will also be dramatically enhanced as well as your ability to learn, grow and have a more refined, poised temperament. You will have a stronger connection with your guardian angel and will likely be able to decipher messages it offers. Your intuitive ability as well as your capacity to discern what is healthy and unhealthy for you will become exceedingly sharpened.

Learning about higher worlds has the potential to shift you from self-pity, depression or a constant self-centredness to a life of service and wisdom, as opposed to a life of living on the surface and wondering what being here is all about.

This type of learning will awaken immeasurable inner richness and desire for progressive evolution. You will also be able to hold and understand the most complex, hidden mystery knowledge, which will strengthen your soul and awaken eternal qualities inside your spirit, deeply fortifying your I am and awakening an ability for your own spiritual research.

On the other hand, if we choose to only focus on this one life and what is happening now and how we can get the most out of it, with very little attention on the detailed, distinct understanding of the spiritual world and the spiritual beings that reside there, our time after death is likely to be increasingly unconscious. In fact, we could become earth bound for a prolonged period and instead of moving forward and evolving, create great destruction on earth, working with beings who want to halt evolution because we want to hold on to what we know.

We are also likely to return to earth with a variety of physical, mental and emotional ailments, difficulty with concentrating, taking positive actions, learning and growing.

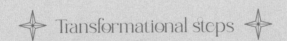

✦ Transformational steps ✦

Think back through this life and all the challenges you have had to deal with already. Have you learned and grown from them? What have you mastered in this life so far that will allow you to have new possibility of growth in your future lives? Find a place where you won't be disturbed, grab a journal and write down any insights that come to you.

What lessons are you ready to face and grow from that can make you feel more strengthened? Are there relationships or things you have done that are incomplete and require you to heal, let go of, forgive or step up in? Take your time to reflect on those insights. If you have a close friend or a counsellor that you can share with, you may find that you gain deeper wisdom into your past experiences and ideas of how you can grow.

You can either focus on what is temporary and what you can get out of life just for yourself, or you can wake up to a bigger picture and focus on long-term transformation, goodness and care towards others and our planet as well as becoming a more evolved human being. The choice is in your hands.

Soul and spirit exploration

From my studies in this area I have learned that the spirit in each of us is eternal in nature; it cannot get sick, it never dies, it's the part of us that incarnates into the physical body one life after another.

The soul divine in its origins also incarnates into a physical body but can get completely absorbed in earthly materialism and its bodily, animal-like nature. The soul can suffer sickness and egoism as it is a part of the astral body. It is where we experience consciousness, feelings, will impulses, sensations and desires. The way that the soul can expand is by uniting with the spirit by absorbing divine truths and goodness. The soul can then become conscious of the world beyond the senses.

The world of the spirit is the setting behind everything that is part of creation, yet it is likely that the spirit in us will remain dormant unless the soul does the inner work to wake it up. When an awakening occurs, the spirit and the higher faculties of soul become united in our divine nature, which is part of earth-human evolution.

We must try to understand with compassion that certain souls will refuse higher knowledge in a particular life or in many lives and will choose to act in a hurtful manner towards others. Thus, their spirit, which still shines, will remain hidden away and unconscious. I truly believe that we must strive and work to refine our soul and connect with our spirit which forms our higher self.

I won't lie, it's not easy, but if you choose to do it, you will potentially access immense higher wisdom and move towards becoming a truly enlightened, wise, loving being who can awaken many others.

✦ Transformational steps ✦

Some of the steps that are required to evolve our soul is to learn patience, kindness, respect, open-mindedness and open-heartedness, inner flexibility, deeper long-term thinking and positivity.

Start with one of the aspects that are mentioned above and give yourself three months to truly focus on this. If for instance you choose patience, focus on mastering patience in every area of life. Take deep breaths in and out when you become overwhelmed and work on responding instead of reacting to life's situations. Recognise that there is divine timing and order in all of life. Whatever aspect you choose to work with you are likely to be tested in. Do not give up because you are uncomfortable, in fact use every opportunity to face your shadow qualities and to grow.

What nourishes and refines the soul

What food is to the body feelings are to the soul. We nourish the soul with feelings of reverence, respect, kindness and devotion.

This makes the soul healthy and strong – particularly for that activity of understanding deeper wisdom.

Judgemental, harsh, critical behaviours paralyse and distort the soul's capacity to refine. However, it is vital that we develop objectivity and discernment around what is healthy for us to experience and what is not.

When a soul is nourished by seeing the good in the most difficult situations and most unpleasant people, the colours in our aura change from brownish red to bluish red.

Our sensitivity and awareness increase and we receive incredible insights from our environment which we were previously unaware of.

Every honourable act, reverence, respect, devotion, love, beauty, kindness, selflessness, warmth, generosity, sensitivity, humility, grace and compassion strengthen our soul and creates eternal qualities that we can take with us through many incarnations. When developed these qualities give us vitality, dynamism, potency and capacities for honesty, integrity and the type of leadership that comes from kindness, goodness and wisdom. They also give us the possibility to return to earth with strengthened bodies that are full of vitality and have a great capacity to regenerate.

Our soul is also uplifted by nature, beautiful artwork, music, stories, architecture, inspiring movement, dance and drama. We can also enhance our soul capacities through discovering more about the stars and studying how the planets, the sun and the moon influence our inner being.

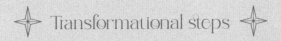

Read through the eternal qualities on the previous page which strengthen the soul. Pick a quality you would like to explore and where you feel you have more possibility for growth.

Take some paper and pencils and create an image that can have words attached to it and represents this quality. Imagine how this quality transforms you as you use it in the future. Who do you become? What possible life experiences can you invite into your life which would be of benefit to you and others?

Why do we
need sleep?

We need to start to understand that we don't sleep simply to rest. We sleep so we can gain the strength we need from the spirit world in order to fulfil our purpose here.

If we live in harmony with others and our inner self – work on deepening our understanding of the hidden world around us, meditate, and are willing to lovingly and at times selflessly be of service – we will find that our connection to the divine grows. We will experience deeper and more nourishing sleep and receive new and inspiring insights and inner strength to co-create our reality.

If we only concentrate on ourselves and how nothing is going right, complain, drink, take drugs, mainly focus on how we can get what we want and act in selfish ways, then our connection will diminish and we will grow more confused, lost and anxious as we grow older. We are also likely to wake up tired, heavy and frustrated. The more we hold on to the material world for our sense of safety, the more likely we are to develop a great fear of the spiritual.

It can also be difficult to let go of the physical world and allow ourselves to vulnerably enter the spiritual world that we know nothing about at a time of crossing over. The more fear we have of what we don't know the more we will try to hold on to what feels safe.

What is important is to slowly explore spiritual ideas and think into them logically while being grounded and connected with your life.

I want to emphasise that I am not saying to let go of full participation in your life, just that it's vital we start to stretch our mind and recognise that there is much more than what we have been taught about.

✦ Transformational steps ✦

Do you have a daily practice? What do you do when you wake up to strengthen your connection to the divine? What do you do during the day to be able to respond and function well when challenges arise? What do you do in the evening in order to create a beautiful sleep?

It is important that you find a practice that works for you. The first step could be learning to tune in to yourself and create a loving environment within.

I suggest you explore the self-love process at the end of this book.

What actually happens during sleep?

When you think into it deeply, sleep can be seen as a mini death. The big question is, where does our consciousness go when we fall asleep?

We need to firstly understand that the astral body gives consciousness to the physical and etheric bodies. Every night during dreamless sleep, the astral and ego body leave to go on a journey into the spirit realm, while the physical and etheric bodies are left lying in bed.

During dreamless sleep we don't feel any joy or sorrow, pain or pleasure or have any mental images and ideas as the astral body is the vehicle for all these things.

Dreamless sleep is a blank in the memory bank of our life because we are unconscious.

Dreaming on the other hand is an intermediate stage between sleeping and waking. We dream when the astral body has separated from the physical, which is why we can't use our senses properly. But because the astral body is still connected to the etheric, it can creatively put images into our brains causing us to dream. Our angel can also give us important messages by creatively imprinting symbolic images into our astral body while we sleep. The more we recognise these messages, the more we feel in alignment with our soul's purpose.

We feel fatigue because the astral body wants to go back into its home of soul and spirit in order to regenerate. During the day we are conscious and the astral body is given over to outer impressions. In sleep the astral body is unconscious and surrounded in its own bodily nature of soul and spirit. This beautiful rhythm of the astral body makes for a healthy life.

The physical body is made of earth and can't live away from the nourishment of earth. The astral body's home is the astral realm and it can't live in the body for long periods of time before it needs to go back to its home. The same divinity that gave birth to the human being gives the astral body the images it needs to nourish the etheric body, which can then maintain the physical body for another day.

The process of going to sleep has massive effects on our everyday life. Every night we are surrounded by spiritual beings: the angels, archangels and the archai. They help us on our journey of development and the fulfilment of our karma. We can become more conscious of the phenomenon of sleep with some deeper understanding and appreciation for its holiness.

Our ego is the youngest member of our being; in waking consciousness it is in a baby state. We mostly have a vague feeling of what the I could be. Most people think of the ego in terms of egotism, however, when we develop a deeper understanding of it, we realise it has two aspects: the lower self, which is only interested in what it can gain for itself in the physical world and the higher self, which awakens when we are willing to live life from a place of service.

The ego comes into a more mature form while we are asleep. If we have been living our life from a space of wisdom it resembles its next future stage of evolution which is spirit self.

Our angels who guide and hold our past lives and our higher self have already reached spirit self so you can see that we are amidst holiness during sleep. With the right type of training this wonderful rhythm of waking and sleeping can become an enriching health-giving connected part of your life.

✦ Transformational steps ✦

Take some time before going to sleep to review your day backwards. Stop at any event that was challenging that day. Do not judge it. Simply ask: what could I have done better? Allow yourself to explore at least one or more options, then keep going.

Exercises like this allow you to respond in a new way a lot more often in your daily life as opposed to reacting based on what you have always done.

Sleep and the transformation of earth

Every day when you wake up you have consciousness and each night when you fall into a deep sleep you lose it.

Throughout the day you have countless thoughts that leave their residue in your physical and etheric bodies. You would not be able to remember any of your earthly life experiences if these traces of memory were not left in your etheric body.

As the etheric lays in bed these traces take on a mysterious process. All your thoughts from waking to sleep begin to move and swirl ringing on waves of sound.

Imagine a certain part of the earth where everyone is sleeping. Picture all these sleeping etheric bodies expressing the previous day's experience. Envisage what weaves in their etheric bodies as an echo of all that they have been thinking during the day. Now picture the beings that hover over those sleeping bodies, rising and descending, busying themselves with the traces of thoughts humming from their etheric bodies. These beings are angels, archangels and the archai. Your sleep is their field of business. Your daily thoughts absorb their attention.

The angels, archangels and archai gather the fruits of your thoughts and carry them up into the Akashic records where they find their place in the cosmic order of life.

Understanding this can help you to reflect deeper and become more conscious.

It can be mind-blowing to realise that our thoughts have a major impact on our future lives. The quality of our thoughts and feelings, our moral inner life, has the power to impact the physical substance of our earth.

The question is will it be transformed into something beautiful, because we have learned to be conscious and taken responsibility for our thoughts, words, feelings and actions and we are willing to give more than we take? Or is the earth going to be altered into something dark and ugly, because our thirst for power, money, sex and control has ruled us?

I am not saying that we don't need money or a sense of accomplishment; however, in earth's vast history, we can see how greed and the need for more influence and control has created division, conflict and great pain.

✦ Transformational steps ✦

What would it be like if even one tenth of the world's population started to deeply care both about treating our planet with reverence and respect and creating a loving, kind, thoughtful community?

Take some time to really reflect on what kind of community you would like to live in and if you have children what you would like them be a part of.

Grab some pencils and paper and draw what it may look like. Then write underneath what you envision. In the next week, share your vision with a few people.

What can you practically contribute to creating the kind of society or community that you would love to live in? Make a list.

Before something comes into a physical reality, it starts as a thought and an idea. What if more of us focused our energy, attention and skill on envisioning and then creating the kind of reality that would inspire us to live in?

Exploring multiple earth lives and karma

Not everyone is comfortable with talking about multiple earth lives and karma. A huge reason is that we have been brainwashed to only believe in the one-life mentality!

This belief, more than anything, creates incredibly destructive behaviour. I mean if you knew you had many lives and that each of your actions shaped your emotional, mental and physical body for the future, let alone the environment you would be born into and your state of health and ability to heal or not, do you think that your actions would be slightly different? Would you be motivated to learn and truly become your best self?

If a person doesn't know this and has only thoughts about one life then they would feel depressed, anxious and fearful about what happens to them when they cross the gate of death and try to cover up those feelings with all types of addictions and control. Or they may take a different stance and try to live their life to the fullest focusing on getting as much stuff, fun and so-called outer success as possible!

In either of these scenarios there is no room to work on the enrichment of your inner life unless you got sick or experienced major trauma and disappointment, which is happening to more and more people.

Awakening your soul requires time, understanding, a consistent self-inquiry and a profound willingness to learn and, more importantly, to create change.

But let's break down the one-life mentality further. We would have to believe that life is totally random and materialistic. That the people we meet have little meaning to us and it really doesn't matter how we treat them as we are going to die and have nothing to do with them once the relationship or this life is over. We might as well treat them badly – lie, cheat and steal as there are no repercussions anyway (or so the one-life proponents want us to believe).

This is opposed to developing the understanding that we have soul families with whom we share many lives and a particular karma. And this is where our greatest growth and evolution might lie. We meet these soul families on our travels through reincarnation again and again and again, in different bodies at different times. This is why when we meet someone from our soul group we experience an often instant connection with them.

If we are to only focus on the one-life paradigm we would have to believe that any ability we have gained in this life would be wasted.

So how do we explain our varied personalities even if we are a twin or a triplet? We have spent the same amount of time in our mother's womb, had the same stimulus yet we are so different. We can't exactly put it all on genetics. How do we explain that a three-year-old can play the piano better than a 50-year-old with huge experience? What about the fact that we are all born with different capacities – one person is amazing at maths and doesn't have anyone in their family to match that ability and another person is an incredible artist and was inspired to start painting when they were five years old? How about all the kids who have never heard about multiple earth lives yet can tell their parents and other adults in detail who they were and what happened to them in a previous life and even know how to speak or understand a different language which they have never learned in this life? Should we ignore all this and hold on to the materialistic point of view that we are only going to have one chance?

Let's go further. No karma means no evolution. If that would be the case we would look back 2000, 5000, 10,000 years and see that people were exactly the same. Yet we can look back as far as 30 years and see the enormous changes that have occurred, let alone understand what people were like in the Egyptian time when they built pyramids or in the time of Atlantis.

However, we also have so many people who want to simplify everything; they market themselves as being super special and say that they can help you to instantly take back your supernatural abilities from those long-gone epochs and reclaim all your clairvoyance. This is one of the things that makes the non-believers point their fingers and look down on anyone who is trying to discuss the importance of understanding multiple earth lives.

Of course those who want to simplify things don't understand that people's souls evolve over time, for example the souls of people in Atlantean or Lemurian times were completely different to the development that our souls are going through now! If we really studied this, we would realise that while we can become a lot more enriched by understanding the past, we cannot bring the past into the future. And the real question is why would we want to do that, as opposed to investing our time into developing something fresh for the future? Can you imagine how many aspects of you are capable of being refined and advanced to something new?

How exciting would it be to develop new faculties by refining the talents we already have and allowing them to flourish into something new? The question is: are you willing to put the work into a potential new discovery or do you feel comfortable with repeating the old? Even if you are born with an amazing ability to sing, you may still require singing lessons in order to know what you are doing and to hone your skills. While honing these skills you might find a new technique which is more efficient and effective than what has previously been taught. Why can't we see that if we come here with special clairvoyant capacities, that we would also need to work on enhancing those and taking them to a new level?

What I'm saying requires a different type of thinking. It opens the door to true soul depth.

I think a majority of us have experienced band-aid solutions and quick fixes. I believe that many souls are yearning for true spiritual depth and evolution as opposed to the fluffy feel-good ideas that leave you in the same confused, numbed state where you started.

When you consider multiple earth lives, you also start to contemplate that your family and in particular your children in this life could have been your siblings, friends, parents, co-workers or partners in other lives. We start to see each person as a soul and a spirit who has their own destiny as opposed to someone we gave birth to that belongs to us.

This awareness frees both you and the other to live the life that is in each person's individual destiny to journey.

✦ Transformational steps ✦

Make a list of all the people and events that have impacted your life the most. Next to each one write down what you have learned and how it has made you grow. Become aware of any unfinished business that you may need to work on. Also look for repetitive patterns that have occurred in your life – this will give you lots of insight about your karmic journey and where you need to keep growing.

Take some time to recognise what gift(s) you naturally possess. If it's more than one, pick what you feel you are ready to refine, it could be anything from your capacity to concentrate, your intuition, writing, singing, cooking, playing an instrument, gardening, painting, astrology, healing and so on and think about what you are willing to do to refine it. Are you willing to study, practice, read about it, take lessons and so on? I encourage you to give yourself an opportunity to use what you were born with or brought from another life and refine it so it can be birthed into a new capacity.

Asking
questions

s we live in the age of technology and have access to
so much information which is often confusing and
contradictory, we need to develop discernment
and the courage to question things, especially
when it has to do with spiritual understanding,
new healing modalities or new practitioners.

We must ask: where does this information come from? Is it based
on profound research that can connect many threads together and
answer important questions, or does this come from someone who
has channelled information from a being they know nothing about?
Is it from a person who has done a couple of 2-3 day courses and now
believes that they can teach and heal?

To be conservative and to do the proper amount of work before you help others has nothing to do with fear and everything to do with ethical responsibility. After all you have the capacity to deeply influence another's life. I know there is a new tendency that has arisen in the New Age community to say, 'If it's meant to be, it's meant to be!' I don't want to offend people, but in a higher reality we are absolutely responsible for how we impact others. Every action we do has a reaction that either leads us towards becoming a more virtuous person or creating a karmic situation for ourselves in the future.

In terms of health the questions you may like to explore when finding someone to work with are: what do they understand about the physical body, food, emotions, beliefs and so on? It can also be helpful to understand which foods affect specific parts of the body and which foods affect the soul. (I tried a particular detox plan and couldn't think or meditate during it as I was eating potatoes every day. It took me a while to realise that it's not an ideal food for developing your concentration and meditation.) We must become conscious of what is important to us. If you spent months or years sensitising yourself then it is vital that you realise what food, drink, TV shows, technology, interactions with others can deaden you.

Obviously there are many things to be aware of. When you see a practitioner you may like to ask whether they understand that you have several energy bodies. Can they describe what is the astral, etheric, mental, emotional and ego body? Are they aware of the difference between the soul and the spirit?

Do they understand the chakra system and the difference between astral and etheric chakras? Have they spent any time developing and understanding how the body sends you messages besides the obvious?

Do they understand what impact occurs in the womb and the first seven years of life? Are they aware of the difference between the ancestral and the karmatic aspects of mental, emotional and physical health and so on?

If they do, they have truly studied! If they don't, it doesn't mean they are not an excellent practitioner, but they may only be able to help you with certain aspects of your well-being. This places you into a space of realistic expectations.

In terms of the spiritual teaching, you may like to explore whether they are teaching about the development of your I am and your spirit or are they still preaching an old paradigm of a group soul mentality – talking about going back into oneness, focusing fervently on the group as opposed to your individual evolution. Please don't misinterpret this as egotism and lack of care for a community.

We need to understand that we are all unique beings and that when we develop our sense of I am, we also develop a capacity to truly think for ourselves as opposed to following what we are told to do by others.

It can also be useful to explore whether a spiritual teacher you choose to learn from has any insight into the planetary stages of evolution of earth. Can they give you any insight into what happened in Lemuria, Atlantis and the various epochs that followed and how our souls developed? Can they explain why the different spiritual and religious impulses came about in different regions and why? Can they help you understand what happens when you pass over and explain the beings that work in the astral worlds or the different aspects of the spiritual world and how that relates to your life now and what you need to work on? Can they give you a glimpse into what karma is in detail and how we create it?

If those important questions and others can be answered then you know this person or people have some profound understandings and you can learn much from them. And please believe me there are quite a few people who really do know what they are talking about. But we need to know what questions to ask in order to find out!

Transformational steps

Reflect on which aspect of life you need more help and support in. Do some research to find someone who can assist you. Take some time to contemplate the questions you need to ask in order to gain deeper wisdom around the topic you need support with. If this person can help you, then explore going on a journey of learning and healing with them, if they cannot then look for someone who has the depth you need. Always reflect internally whether what you are learning truly resonates with you.

Is it wise to question your spiritual explorations?

I'm not writing this to offend as your truth can serve you at different points in your life. I'm writing this because I believe that we need to start to think in a more logical way and question things as opposed to believe anything that shows up that sounds spiritual, instant and almost magical.

Not all beings who people can connect with are coming from a higher place of evolution. They may give you the messages you want to hear of self-love and appear like they come from the light only to teach you confusing half-truths that actually blind you, make your soul empty, full of pride and block your progress.

From the time I first started working with people I have perceived a type of soul numbness in countless people. It's taken me years to understand where it comes from and the consequences of it. (I also saw it in myself for years not knowing how to transform it.)

The consequences of soul numbness are very serious as on a mental level it places you in a loop where you can't learn information that can challenge and stretch you. You stay in the comfort zone of your beliefs. These could be either heavy, negative, victim-like or they could be the opposite – that all is light, beautiful and wonderful and we can instantly heal and change anything. Both of those extremes miss many details or actual understanding of the process of development of our soul and spirit, higher and lower spiritual beings and where we are at in the evolution of humanity let alone any real understanding of how karma works and what occurs during our time in the spiritual worlds.

On an emotional level soul numbness leads to either depression, suppression, fear, disassociation, confusion or emptiness. It also affects our memory and our ability to function optimally or to feel emotions. It can lead us into anxiety where we become too emotional, angry, enraged, prideful, selfish, manic, overexcited and delusional. This can create a constant focus on achieving pleasure, enlightenment and bliss instantly with no real work on self.

This is where so many people get tempted into the world of plant medicines as it's easy and requires no inner refinement or preparation. Just by letting go of their I am and entering into lower astral worlds they know nothing about, they tear apart their etheric body with the idea that they are clearing all their ancestral memories; however, what they don't realise is that everything has its price. For you to enter into a realm you have not worked for and not been invited to, you have to give an aspect of your soul to the beings of that world and take on something of theirs.

I've seen many people who have gone on those journeys and returned ungrounded, full of entities, and with nervous system dysfunctions. Some have also shared their reliance on plant medicine to do self-discovery and shadow work. The challenge of using substances which are connected to beings you know nothing about is that you would not know how to truly discern if what you are being shown is the truth and whether you are connecting to higher beings or lower beings that are posing as beings of love and light.

So the question is, can plant medicine open spiritual doors? From my observation it looks a little more like knocking those doors down. I guess the real question for each individual is, do you truly believe that you can push yourself into the higher worlds unprepared and be completely safe or would you prefer to learn, discover, work on your shadow consciously and then be invited into the spiritual realm because you are ready?

I can hear your argument about people who have done those practices and how they discovered things about themselves and healed and connected to their hearts and now feel love. I am not denying that this is possible and for certain people the journey can be helpful at a particular moment in their life. Yet there is still a question of what is the price of short cuts? Anything that weakens your inner self and puts it into a sleepy state where someone else takes over without you being consciously in charge of yourself can have major side effects.

Again, I am here just to stretch your mind and make you question things you may not have questioned previously, therefore I ask you to explore, either from your own experiences or those who have dabbled into them, and think on how this process has helped you as well as numbed and deadened you or this person. Has it made you or them believe that you don't really have to go on a profound journey to understand, discover and discern the higher beings from the darker? How has this easy trip stopped a person's inner development and the understanding of what really happens when in higher spiritual worlds?

Do you really believe that angels, archangels, the archi, exusiai, kyriotetes, seraphim, cherubim and so on wanted us to take drugs or medicine to understand spiritual realms? Or did they want us to refine, ennoble and purify ourselves and do the work that makes us grow into incredible human beings?

Is it therefore possible that the beings who do want you to have instant experiences are playing on the other side? Only you can come to a true discernment of this if you choose to take the time to think it through.

I am aware that saying this can upset some people. If you are a person who is upset by this, ask yourself if the reason you feel uncomfortable is because maybe you are resonating with something in what I am saying?

I'm a little passionate about this subject as you can gather. I constantly receive private messages about the damage these 'medicines' cause people. And this potential damage is not just to the physical body, which is temporary, but to the soul and the spirit which have long-term consequences for possibly many lifetimes. But again we are free to believe, do and follow whatever we desire!

I can't count how many times I've heard, 'We are connecting to the healing aspect of Gaia or Mother Earth' yet the people who say this have done no research on the real beings who live inside the various layers of the earth. And not all of them are loving. Think of all the wars that have been fought and the trauma inside Gaia!

Ignorance can be bliss at first but eventually there is a price for that ignorance. I have learned this lesson in a painful way so many times.

On a physical level if you have soul numbness your soul which houses your astral body becomes lazy. The astral body is connected to your nervous system and is the body which sends messages to every part of your being on what to do, therefore, as you can imagine in soul numbness the messages being sent are not necessarily the right ones or the ones that are the most helpful. This leads to a host of different diseases and a disconnection from ourselves and of course a desire to be instantly saved.

If my soul is weak and my sense of self (I am) is weak then what are my chances of true self-healing and transformation? Let alone a connection to my higher self.

I know this is not easy to digest but from what I have learned, spiritual half-truths which circulate in the New Age world can be incredibly damaging. This is not just about eating the wrong food and then doing a detox. This is about how your soul is affected and what the consequences are for your potential for evolution.

Let's use some logic here. In our present world almost every person is channelling and those who are have very little understanding of the energy bodies and what impact that has; for example, channelling a being who you don't understand, who comes from a realm you know nothing about can separate and weaken your etheric (life) body and suppress your I. And then this being, who is potentially interfering in the human experience, gets to live through your body and influence all your thoughts. You may even become a lot smarter and business savvy but at the same time lose your independence.

There are people claiming that every evolved master or group of masters including God and Christ are channelling through them. Yet I'm wondering why a highly evolved being would need to channel through someone, as that means that they have to take over their body and push out their I. And why would an evolved being possess someone who has not followed any of the spiritual laws and is completely unprepared for higher knowledge and may live their life in a very egotistical way?

If we could just be possessed, it would show that we are living at a time of no free will! In fact, I'm talking from quite a bit of experience of both seeing, doing and tuning in to the process of channelling, which to my spiritual vision looks like someone is trespassing into another's holy space.

But more than anything it deeply concerns me that so many people have now been taught that they are not required to do the earnest work of getting to know themselves, meeting their shadow aspects as well as their light, learning about their spiritual nature and being genuinely good people. None of which is easy and all of which requires a lot of time and effort.

My half a lifetime of research tells me that if you don't have to evolve and work on things and it's instant and easy, then what you are connecting to is far from the higher beings.

Of course, I must keep emphasising we are all free to believe what we want. That is what freedom is about. What I'm encouraging is for you to think deeply and use your logic.

Don't just believe me, do your own research. Many of us including myself have been lured into get rich schemes only to lose our hard-earned money and our pride. Most of us have also experienced con artists in personal relationships as well as working ones. The spiritual industry is full of traps and people who genuinely believe that what they do helps but who have never truly taken the time to question what they are receiving and from whom.

There is a lot of magical thinking and miraculous type mentality. If it sounds too good to be true with no real work required, then maybe it is. And maybe there are also great side effects to that which we don't yet know about.

✦ Transformational steps ✦

Take an opportunity to develop your discernment by giving yourself permission to be honest with yourself and ask hard questions. What do you believe about your healing journey? Do you think it should be instant with no effort or do you feel that getting to know yourself requires you to be conscious, awake and willing to meet all your challenges head on? What have you tried that worked for you? Did it make you truly grow, or did it seem like you were growing but you were actually stunted? Where are you at in your life now in terms of your interest, willingness and desire to grow? Take some time to contemplate what is important for you at present.

Why higher beings will not give knowledge to those who are unprepared

I am exploring these questions in order to encourage you to discern what you want to feed your soul with, as now more than ever we have so many people sharing an array of spiritual truths. We need to look a little further before we hand our trust over to someone who makes life sound easy, pleasing and appealing, especially if they have written some popular books.

The first question I ask is: what did they have to do to acquire the abilities they have in order to communicate with higher spiritual beings?

This is obviously a very delicate subject so I'm going to share my journey. When I awakened my intuition to tune in to people at a young age, I assumed that all I had to do was use this ability and I would get better. I didn't understand that just as there are physical laws – for example, we stop at the red light or we will hurt ourselves and others – there are also profound spiritual laws that require deep preparation in order to receive accurate (this is the emphasis) spiritual perceptions.

Let's look at this in more detail. From many, many years of research and mistakes that almost cost me my sanity, I now understand that to receive genuine spiritual insights we first must work on our lower self. This means that we need to spend time getting to know our numbed, hidden, suppressed, highly shameful shadow side. I say shameful because shame is what makes us hide and become unconscious of our darker aspects.

To enter spiritual worlds without doing the deep work of looking at this part of ourselves means that everything we will see will be perceived through the reflection of this shadow self. (And working on your shadow requires some deep courage!)

Let's go further. There is a reason that in the past there were many mystery centres who hid the higher truths from the public because, unlike popular teachers, they would make us believe higher wisdom is not just a few simple words about love and peace but a very intricate process of inner transformation. Higher wisdom actually requires us to understand that our soul has gone through many stages of evolution.

We are not the same as we were in the time when Egypt, Greece or Indian civilisations were at their peaks. What we could do in Egypt when we built the pyramids is unfathomable to us in our time. Instead, we are in a time of technological advancement.

If we delve into what higher wisdom is, it may require us to learn where we are at in our evolution and why and it may ask us to become curious about the different aspects of the soul and the spirit awakening. Understanding this gives us hope as well as a clearer vision of what we need to work on for the present and for the future.

From my research every higher spiritual perception that you receive which is accurate requires you to take three moral steps forward. These moral steps forward need to be objective. Meaning that most people around you who live by an ethical code would agree that those steps are coming from a deep place of goodness and love for others.

For some this can be far from easy! For instance, when people become known or have huge success they are often given permission to behave however they like. Look at the music or film industry. Idolisation doesn't usually lead to good things. In the past actors used to be the most evolved bringers of the higher truths.

So why does it not make sense that anyone who desires it would just be able to connect to angelic, archangelic, archi and even higher beings and receive higher wisdom? Because from what I understand higher wisdom requires a higher level of responsibility and thus deeper preparation. It is easy to use higher wisdom for our own power and aggrandisement as we have seen many do as opposed to really serving humanity.

Higher beings are wise and generally do not give great power to those who are likely to abuse it but lower-level beings are likely to be there in an instant to give you so-called higher confused knowledge – although it's always for a price even if you are not aware that you are paying.

More evolved beings would never take over your body; they would give you the freedom to listen to them with your sense of self or I am being intact. If your body is taken over, your capacity for discernment diminishes greatly, thus how do you really know who is speaking through you?

So, what did I personally learn? I learned that since I didn't have to work for it, I used my abilities as much as I could but in the process I dulled my soul and ended up feeling empty for years. While I was under the impression that I was growing, my higher self was trying to wake me up.

As far as abilities go, as much as I was excited by my accuracy and capacity to tune in and help others, this was like baby steps compared to what I believe we are all capable of. While I may have earnt those intuitive capacities in earlier lives, I learned the hard way that you cannot use the old in a new time without refining it.

I only woke up when I stopped travelling and had some time to go within and begin to discover more of who I am. The most shocking thing was that I had believed I was so deep, yet in truth I had many holes that I needed to work on in order to refine and strengthen myself and become wiser – and the more I learn, the more I know there is a lot more to learn.

I can't say that waking up and looking in the mirror has been an easy process but as challenging as it has been I now rise every day with a soul that is full of life, vitality and a high willingness to learn and apply new wisdom as much as I'm capable. (Not that I'm not constantly presented by challenges and awarenesses of how my lower self functions.)

Has my intuition transformed? Let's just say that my ability to discern what comes from those who have spent many years of self-refinement as opposed to the people who make things sound wonderful but have not done any real work on themselves to awaken the petals of their heart and other chakras through a daily practice is stronger.

Also my sensitivity and ability to feel a rainbow of colourful emotions as opposed to just the intensity of the big ones has been heightened. And the depth I am finally feeling in my soul, as well as the heart connection I have developed with many people, is worth more to me than any physical riches.

Just as we need to discern what food, company, work and entertainment is good for us in the physical world, we also need to start to discern what is important for our soul and the growth of our spirit by the type of spiritual truths we nourish it with.

For instance, there are many people who teach that angels and archangels are equivalent to genies who will fulfil our every wish if we are just willing to ask. Yet if we truly think into it, we might start to question this particularly pleasant but not very accurate description of their role. In our questioning, we may discover a deeper truth of what these beings and others even more evolved than they are do for humanity – I wrote about this earlier.

We can then actually begin to feel true awe for our life and start to live differently to just surviving and getting as many things as we can that make us comfortable. We would stop being so obsessed by everything that is physical while at the same time deeply valuing our bodies and lives.

I believe my role is not necessarily to give you all the answers, as that is a personal journey, but I do feel a strong responsibility to make you think and to keep asking questions! As it's in the quality of the questions that we ask that we have the possibility for our deepest growth.

✦ Transformational steps ✦

Is there an ability you have that you would like to develop further? Is it something that you find difficult or something that comes easily to you? If it is something challenging, what are you required to face? If it is something that is natural to you, how can you take it to another level? I encourage you to keep asking questions and allowing yourself to research and learn more about who you are as well as to truly embrace the challenges as well as the joys in your life, seeing the blessings of both.

SPIRITUAL AWAKENING, INTUITION AND INNER MASTERY

The deeper path to spiritual evolution and awakening your intuition

I believe there are both safe and dangerous paths towards spiritual awakening. The safer path is longer, involves deeper work and encourages profound understanding and discernment, but most importantly it asks you to take the time required to develop proper spiritual organs of perception. This process is unique and different for each person.

Think about it. How clear, precise and consistent can your intuition be if you have never spent the time required to create a proper organ of perception? As you can imagine if you think into it, to develop acute spiritual vision and hearing isn't instant. It takes effort even if you have already awakened those capacities to some degree.

Now let's imagine that an aspect of your soul has begun to awaken but it's early days and without the ability to truly hear or see you push it into exploring spiritual worlds with minimal understanding of how they work. Would that not be equivalent to putting a person into the middle of a forest who is blind and deaf and asking him/her to find their way home?

My personal experience is that if you rush to awaken these faculties in yourself too quickly there are huge consequences to that – from eventual mental, energetic and physical breakdowns to massive issues in your astral body which if you don't know how to work and refine can literally turn into an emotional beast of selfishness, egotism and desire without you even really noticing it.

Let's go into a deeper exploration of entering spiritual worlds through using fast and easy methods.

How can it be a real evolving journey if you weaken your sense of self or I am and lose your conscience while giving your power to someone else who is supposedly looking after your soul while you go on a trip into a realm you haven't learned about nor truly understand?

Have you worked on anything in yourself to get there or was the medicine, drug or someone else the way in?

Think about it: are you likely to truly see the spiritual world you know nothing about or are you more likely to see a reflection of your lower self and your ideas of the spiritual world? (Which for some who only believe in the physical reality can be somewhat helpful and even awakening yet some of the side effects are tearing your soul, creating holes in your etheric body, potential disassociation from the physical body, illusions and delusions, ungroundedness, nervous system disorders, potential mental illness and a host of other issues.)

The other point I keep repeating as I want people to think about it is, why would higher beings connect to a person who has not worked on refining their astral body?

I feel like we have had so much confusing information of quick ways to get to everything that we have stopped really thinking about what makes logical sense.

When we begin our journey either way can be helpful – even if it's not the highest way the danger is that we don't develop the inner depth required to find a way that truly feeds our spirit and allows us to grow to our potential.

The surface ways are everywhere and they look easy and appealing and if we haven't experienced a longer, deeper and more profound way we really can't tell the difference. (This was a huge revelation for me. What I thought was deep in the past was just skating the surface.)

This is not to criticise various ways that people do things but to make you think into where you are and ask what you would truly love to experience.

At the end of the day we do not leave this earth with any earthly riches, only with the inner richness we have accumulated.

A great question to ask is: how much of what I have spent my time gathering is valuable for my experience in higher worlds and future lives and how much is destructive or will simply disappear after this life is gone?

I mean, are you going to be worrying about paying your bills or your car on your death bed?

✦ Transformational steps ✦

So how might a slower path look? One that involves a willingness to slow down and listen to your inner being or working towards strengthening your physical, mental, emotional and spiritual well-being? This usually involves giving up anything that leads to a destruction of the body.

Clear calm thinking, steadfastness and an inner stability are essential towards developing your intuition. Having the courage to look at your shadow aspects and face them is also incredibly important. Confidence in your capacity to competently deal with whatever challenge life provides you with builds your inner strength and groundedness, which leads to both open-mindedness as well as discernment.

Working on your empathy as well as learning to take responsibility for your actions and how you show up and make a difference to others combined with taking time out to truly work on transforming your weaknesses into strength.

Becoming aware that your thoughts and feelings are just as important as your words and actions and that anything you do to refine yourself also impacts the world. The world is as much impacted by beautiful thoughts, feelings and words as it is by good deeds. In fact, all good deeds start with good thoughts.

Learn more about your true nature as a soul spiritual being.

Find a way to be of true service to others.

Follow through on the positive resolutions you have made, even if they are difficult, unless they end up hurting others or creating great destruction.

In the higher realms, love, care, kindness and selflessness are the only motivations for actions.

You must be willing to do what is honest, ethical, transformational and uplifting regardless of how it is received by others and whether it is deemed successful by the outer world.

Become full of gratitude and value your connections with others and all the beautiful things that come into your life.

Only when you love someone or something with your whole heart can their true essence be revealed to you. Know deep within your soul that every revelation is a gift of wisdom and enrichment.

These are some of the foundations we need to enter the slower path towards the highest spiritual perceptions. We do not have to be perfect, but we do need to strive to create the kind of inner temple which could inspire higher beings to open the doors to holy wisdom.

Self-mastery

I f we are not masters of our lives but are ruled by life, then the challenges of outer life start to press in on us from all sides, consistently creating an emotional roller coaster and an atmosphere of inner turmoil.

Only by creating a sense of strength in our soul by taking some time out during each day to calmly focus on an aspect of our lives from more objective eyes can we start to develop the possibility to gently awaken our higher self.

Outer circumstances can only change our outer situation, they can never awaken our spirit on their own. Only dedication and the daily inner work of self-refinement with specific exercises can rouse our higher faculties of soul and spirit.

As long as the outer aspect of ourselves is guiding our lives, our innermost sacred self is chained and has no aptitude to unfold its capacities.

So how do you know when you are a step closer to mastering yourself? When you develop the capacity to only be impacted in your inner life by those aspects of your outer life that you choose to consciously allow! This includes all the thoughts and feelings that arise within you. In other words, you become aware, alert and vigilant to what you entertain and feed inside your soul.

When I was travelling around the world I met a very interesting man. When he was younger he had been in a gang and had no belief in anything spiritual until a gun was held to his head. Somehow he survived that ordeal and experienced an awakening. He went home and made a decision to discover the true depth of love. He meditated on love every day for a year. After a year had passed, he realised that no matter how deep he explored there was more love than any human could experience. At that point he also recognised that what was happening in his outer life became irrelevant to him. It didn't matter if he had money or was poor, if he had good health or not, if it was raining or the sun was shining outside, his inner state was not impacted. This birthed true wisdom and groundedness inside him and an ability to face any situation from a space of divine wisdom and love.

If others can make you upset, irritated and angry then you are not yet a master of yourself. If you can look at others with objectivity, empathy and compassion then you will have the possibility to find what is good, lovable and valuable in each human being.

At the same time, be kind to yourself and others; we have many lifetimes to refine ourselves. Work on what comes up step by little step, knowing that self-mastery takes time and it is totally okay to take a few steps back or to the side sometimes. These steps allow you to discover more wisdom and help you to become aware of what you may need to focus on.

We are living at a time where there is much darkness in the world. To turn something murky, ugly and immoral into something that is beneficial, noble and helpful to others is one of the highest virtues we can achieve.

Transformational steps

Spend a whole day observing what triggers you. Explore what the trigger is about. Is it coming from the present or from the past? What aspect of yourself is it asking you to face? What would a response as opposed to a reaction to the trigger look like?

To face yourself

To face oneself means we have to look within, discover and meet those aspects that live and toil in the unconscious recesses of our inner being.

An emotion that I have discovered that can live in the deepest shadow of our being is self-hatred. It operates undercover and only comes out into full view during times of profound humiliation, rejection, abandonment and distress.

This self-hatred began with the smallest incidents when we were little and were ignored by our parents when we wanted to show them our painting or rejected by someone who we looked up to, or hurt and teased by other kids and so on and grows into a beast as the injurious incidents build and we begin the destructive journey of blaming ourselves for everything that went wrong with our parents, siblings and our own lives.

Self-disgust can lead us to the harshest self-criticism and abuse. Consciously or unconsciously we say you have hurt me but I can do it better, harsher, deeper. It is what encourages us to punish, sabotage, inject deadly drugs, hurt, harm, starve ourselves of things we need, put ourselves in situations that suppress our spirit and don't allow us to grow.

At one point in my life I met a man who on the outside was extremely attractive, however, inside he carried immense shame from his childhood where he had been constantly humiliated and was full of self-hatred and rage. Whenever any wonderful opportunities came his way he would make sure that he not only sabotaged them but destroyed the possibilities and everyone involved. He hid his self-hatred by being very charming. He self-punished himself by trying to self-destruct through drugs, sex and becoming a drug dealer. Unfortunately no matter how much he tried, he wasn't able to truly meet himself and instead created a false self that he could hide behind. He read books, taught others, talked about being selfless but could never align his words and actions. Any time he felt under pressure he would become aggressive, violent, controlling and push his shame and self-hatred onto others. This experience with him led me to understand how this inner loathing has the potential to turn into narcissism, psychopathy or sociopathy.

If we keep ignoring our inner shame and hatred we will have a society of people who disassociate, get depressed, need medication or spend most of their lives on drugs, put on huge amounts of weight, become anorexic, develop anxiety and all sorts of phobias, and so on. Mostly they will try to get away in whatever way they can from their pain and the true possibility of growth.

It's not easy to face your inner judge and the covered up self-loathing. I know, as I've avoided the deeper, more painful discoveries as much as anyone. But there is no growth, no true wisdom and no real evolution without the inner work! It was only when I could admit that I had some self-loathing and work on it through journaling, seeing this hateful part of me as an archetype and dancing with it, did I feel that I could embrace it and experience greater self-acceptance and wholeness.

To truly face yourself is the hardest and most rewarding thing you can do. It is only when you take full responsibility – not blame – that you have the choice to recognise all of who you are and start to honour and love all of you that you really grow. As you do that you awaken a higher level of objectivity and true forgiveness for others. Your heart opens but it does so with healthy boundaries. You no longer have a need to put yourself in harmful situations with harsh people. You keep your heart open to them if or when they are ready and willing to heal.

It's easy to see the sense in this, but are you brave enough to look deep or do you prefer to skim the surface trying to convince yourself and everyone else that everything is okay and you are fine and happy?

Light truly shines when we face the darkness, then the darkness can be transformed into the brightest light!

If you do the work you will never get bored, but you will become a much more evolved, aware, understanding and compassionate person.

 Transformational steps

Write down all the aspects of yourself you have placed into the shadow and all that you have placed into the light, but you still disown.

Meet them and invite them to share their wisdom with you. There is so much to discover.

Why resistance and do we need to pay attention?

Of course all profound inner work that makes you face your darkness usually comes with major resistance. This resistance often appears in a guise of fear, self-sabotage and trying to get you out of your body and into your head. In fact, you will know that you are potentially about to hit a breakthrough when you have committed to work with a particularly powerful healing coach or have signed up for a workshop and every part of you wants to run and hide.

So many of us have been taught to look at our feelings as something foreign that needs to be completely controlled or denied. Think of all the times you have been told to stop expressing yourself as a child: don't cry, don't say what you think, don't voice your fears, everything will be fine, be strong, don't be a girl, it's weak to cry and on and on …

This of course can lead to a myriad of mental illnesses or a need to take drugs, watch TV, stay on your phone, eat chocolate and do everything possible to distract yourself from meeting and bringing awareness to your inner life.

At the same time, there are many people who have been teaching us to dive into our emotional life without any real preparation or understanding of what we might meet there.

From my realisation whenever we connect with our feelings we also open the doors to spiritual worlds.

If we don't understand those worlds and the beings that could potentially be influencing us, we could be taken over by our feelings and become lost in the world of non-stop emotions and create all sorts of mental, emotional and physical ailments. This is how people who may have a traumatic experience or an overwhelm of emotions when their I becomes weakened can get stuck in anxiety, regress back to a small child, become depressed, acquire an obsessive compulsive disorder, develop anorexia or bulimia or even become schizophrenic.

There are many things to be aware of before embarking on a deep emotional dive. The first thing to realise is that you are not a victim of your life circumstances. No matter what has happened to you, there is likely to be a karmatic reason for why you must learn this lesson. I'd also like to remind you that karma is not something bad but an opportunity for growth.

This can be very difficult to digest in our culture of abuse; however, if you can expand your point of view out of a one-life paradigm, then you can ask some powerful questions.

I know I am entering into sensitive territory here and I am not saying we should justify abusive behaviour or that we should make up a reason for it to make ourselves feel bad or guilty. What I am saying is that there is a possibility that many of the difficult experiences we have could have a possible karmatic connection.

For instance, could it be possible that if I abuse and hurt people in one life, then in another life I could endure some kind of painful or difficult treatment?

It may not be black and white but there have been enough people who have experienced past life regression and learned that their circumstances in this life as well as their health and the people they meet may have something to do with the experiences they have had in previous lives.

For this reason and others when we embark on deep emotional work we need to make sure that we have a strong sense of self so that we can examine what happened and go on a journey of deep understanding, healing and transformation.

When we work with emotions we need to be willing to comprehend them and the impact they have as well as the wisdom we can gain from them. Our emotions can give us profound insights into how to treat others and the healthy boundaries we need to engage in ourselves.

To go deeper into our inner life we have to be strong and grounded enough to be able to cope with the profound discoveries we are likely to unearth. Some of them can truly shake us to the core as we uncover the truth of how our earlier experiences have impacted every aspect of our lives and caused major pain to ourselves and our loved ones. Therefore, proper rituals of connecting to your I am, accessing your wise self and grounding are vital.

To safely work with our feeling life, which is deeply necessary for the expansion of our inner life, we must understand that we are a thinking, feeling, willing being. We also need to start to familiarise ourselves with the spiritual beings that want to assist us in softening, developing empathy, love, compassion and understanding and those who want to take us into hatred, self-sabotage, fear, egotism and perpetual focus on self and how others have hurt us.

We must be open to continual learning as opposed to becoming ego centric and thinking that we have already understood it all. I am constantly being humbled as I discover new and powerful wisdom that makes me rethink what I thought was my truth and enter a new comprehension of both what is beneficial and what can actually be damaging to our soul and spirit.

When resistance comes up, we may be on the cusp of a huge breakthrough into new facets of understanding ourselves or we could be putting ourselves into a vulnerable position of working with someone who has great intentions but doesn't understand the deeper ramification for the soul if it gets stuck in emotional states that it cannot come out of. This is why I am constantly asking people to be cautious of doing deep emotional work that is harsh or forced as you have no idea what you are actually pulling out of your unconscious and instead work slowly, gently, deeply and with self-kindness.

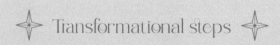

✦ Transformational steps ✦

Before starting any deep emotional work, I encourage you to work with the processes at the end of this book. I suggest starting with the strengthening your I am process, then working with the self-love process and ending with the trauma release process.

Does this mean we should run away from our feeling work?

No! It means that we have to be conscious and responsible, gentle and allowing when we begin to meet, feel and understand our own disowned shadow aspects. We need to learn, befriend and help them grow and transform.

We live at a time when this is not only necessary for our own well-being but it is crucial for the evolution of all of humanity. In meeting and transforming our own darkness we have the possibilities to discover something hidden, surprising and incredibly valuable to us and those around us.

Then, instead of being a person full of empty dark areas that we have to spend an enormous amount of energy protecting, suppressing and ignoring we have an opportunity to creatively channel our newly evolved aspects into much more helpful forms.

For example, if I can see my own hardness, have compassion for these parts of myself that were formed from rejection, fear, neglect, guilt, shame and pride, I can explore them and receive a gift of deeper understanding from them, then great healing can occur – both for myself, my children, other family members, past and present intimate partner(s) and friends.

With regular and gentle connection with my disowned self I can transform what has been dark and unrefined within me for possibly many, many lifetimes into the deepest care, understanding, presence, lovingness, softness, humility and a willingness to listen, learn and discover myself as a much more whole, empowered being.

It's time to consciously open the door to the profound gifts of our feelings and how they can help us become more whole, expressive and enriched.

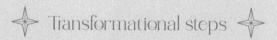

Transformational steps

Spend some time working with the shadow process and forgiveness process at the end of this book.

Healing is an ever-evolving experience

When you first begin your journey into tuning in and discovering what is being held inside your soul, you may uncover deeply unprocessed feelings, traumas and encounters with others that have created hurt, rejection, fear, humiliation and so on.

As you keep exploring you may find that some things, which are either on the surface or you have put a lot of effort into in the past, may heal quickly. Other things may take longer as they are ancestral, tangled in very old patterns, coming from your childhood or even previous lives.

The things that don't heal no matter what you try are usually karmic. They require more than just processing, understanding or clearing something from the past although this could also be important.

The physical or emotional challenges that don't go away need a paradigm shift. You are being asked to prepare yourself for something that is new, potentially quite uncomfortable and deeply personal. You are being asked to look within and develop fierce honesty.

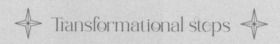 Transformational steps

Some questions to contemplate are: what do I keep doing that is diminishing myself and making me needy, small, fearful and limited? Am I willing to admit to myself that I need to grow?

If you are truly sincere, you will find new opportunities and people coming into your life to both test and help you develop new aspects of yourself.

From my understanding a karmic agreement is what you implanted into yourself with the help of heavenly beings while you were in the spiritual world in between death and rebirth in order to let go of the past and evolve in the deepest ways possible. It's as if you thought: what are the likeliest scenarios where I will have to do something different, learn the most, and become the best person I can be? Then you created your life situations.

Rather than seeing a challenge you are going through or ailments you may have as something that is frustrating and holding you back, you can perceive it as something that requires you to develop deeper inner capacities that motivate you to strive for something higher.

Busily focusing on survival or staying on the surface of life is what makes your life go by and then one day you wake up empty – a shell of what you could have been if you only took the time and had the motivation to know yourself.

If you don't understand multiple earth lives, it becomes incredibly frustrating if your body doesn't heal. But when you start to understand that you are not only working on transforming this life but also your karma from the previous ones and are building the possibilities of a different body and experience for future lives, things become a lot more interesting and motivating.

After all, how would you know what you need to work on if your body and inner self didn't show you?

Evolution is about going beyond your comfort zone and waking up!

Thinking,
feeling, willing

O ur thinking centre is connected to our head, brain and nervous system. This is where we are the most conscious. Our feeling is where we have dreamy consciousness and is connected with the rhythm of our breathing, our heartbeat and the constant flow of blood circulation. Our will is where we have dreamless sleep consciousness and is connected to our limbs, digestion, movement and metabolic system.

When we cross a threshold into the spiritual world through particular meditations, near-death experiences or when we pass over a separation takes place, a kind of differentiation of the soul. The forces of thinking, feeling and willing which are interconnected in the ordinary consciousness become independent from each other. Thinking becomes autonomous, feeling separates and will becomes independent and spreads out like a fan of colour: red in the realm of willing, green in the realm of feelings and yellow in the realm of thinking.

When a person's sense of self or I am is healthy then the interaction between thinking, feeling and willing is so synchronised that they do not fuse into each other but jointly influence each other. The mystery of the I is that when it is developed it maintains thinking, feeling and willing side by side which in turn creates harmony. However, if the I has been weakened through alcohol, drug use, immense strain, trauma, lack of sleep and so on, then thinking can get pushed aside while feeling can engulf both thinking and willing and major confusion can result where the whole organism is seized by emotions.

This occurs when thinking becomes weakened then because the I is not working properly, thinking moves into the sphere of feelings or will and merges with one or both. This is what occurs when people develop anxiety, depression, mania, multiple personality disorder, OCD, PTSD and a host of other mental and emotional conditions. It is vital that we learn how to develop our thinking and hold it apart from the intensity of our emotions and will. Nowadays we are constantly bombarded by so much information, impressions, requests and things to do that it is easy for us to get overwhelmed and allow our feelings to take over.

On the physical plane we are the most conscious of our thinking. Our feelings are dreamy and connected to spiritual beings in the spiritual realms. When we start to work with immense feelings and have a limited or confused understanding of the super-sensible realms of existence we awaken and become confronted with spiritual beings, not all of them of a higher, loving nature. When those beings of anger, fear, depression, anxiety and panic take over we become imprisoned by their darkness and our I continues to diminish. Therefore, we need to start discovering more and more about the spiritual realms. We need to stop accepting generalisations and calling everything energy, and instead understand that our thoughts and feelings are connected to spiritual beings.

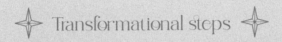

Transformational steps

When we are thinking certain thoughts, feeling certain feelings and participating in particular actions we need to become conscious of what beings we are nourishing.

Simply by identifying a feeling and imagining an archetypal image of this feeling we can become conscious of what potential realities we are creating for ourselves. The more we feed the negative, the more likely we are to develop illness. Suppressing and pretending that lower aspects of you don't exist can lead as much to sickness as constantly swimming in irritation, frustration, rejection, anger and victimhood.

A willingness to learn about spiritual realities from ethical sources, meaning those who have truly researched them, can not only strengthen your I but also your ability to balance thinking, feeling and willing in a healthy way.

Some of us need to work more on our thinking as we act too impulsively and then wonder why things don't work while others have to refine their feeling life as they allow their emotions to take over and lead them into constant conflict.

Why what works at one point in your life may not at another

I t's important for us to understand that what works at one point in our lives might be the very thing that holds us back the most at another.

Being open-minded and teachable is a huge key to evolution.

The beliefs and ideas I had in my early twenties when I first discovered spirituality and healing work were incredibly awakening for my soul. They gave me a purpose and something to hold on to that made me feel better. As I got into my thirties those same ideas, processes and practices made me feel blocked, numb, confused, stuck and empty. But I was so attached to them because they had previously helped me – to change was a real inner struggle. I was extremely fortunate because I have a strong willingness to learn and objectively examine what does and doesn't work. The more I realised how complacent I was becoming because I was wanting the easy path the less creative I became.

Eventually I could no longer stand the emptiness in my soul and the same old ways of thinking and feeling. It was a process, but through intense dedication I began to change my inner life.

Thinking deeply is one of our biggest gifts and the best remedy against Alzheimer's and many other diseases.

Discovering generalised, half-baked theories and concepts that have very limited answers for the most important life questions is easy but you are much more than what you have been led to believe.

I'm constantly getting messages from people who want to heal or awaken their intuition but when I share with them the safe but extensive journey it requires, they move on to the next person who will make promises to them to awaken their higher faculties or heal them instantly with no real effort on their part. (Which, I hate to break it to you, either doesn't work or will make you feel good for a short period of time but doesn't last.)

To awaken and do the real inner work is to bring the spark of the most incredible aliveness into your life. Aliveness that keeps growing and revealing the deeper secrets of our lives.

Do we have to be ready for something new? Yes! Is it going to be blissfully easy to refine your astral body and understand why we are at a time in evolution where there are so many crimes, diseases, dark agendas and sexual abuse? No! But the question is always whether you want to sleep through life and then suffer the consequences, or are you willing to be courageous?

Have you had enough of the old and are now ready to open yourself up to new possibilities and experiences?

I once read a description of evil being something that worked really well at one time in the past and is now being dragged into the present.

As you grow you begin to realise that every month, year and decade you become a new person and open new doors towards discovering yourself. For instance, at one point in your life you may have suppressed your inner child because you've experienced trauma, at another point you decided to work on releasing the charge and healing the trauma and later you were ready to forgive what happened. As you go further you start to reflect on the idea that nothing is random and that we co-create our own reality. You start to ask yourself some big questions, such as what led to that traumatic situation? This may result in you wanting to discover what happens in the spiritual realms and the exploration of past lives and karma and onto the need to understand the hierarchies of the angels. This journey of discovery can lead you towards making changes in how you live and relate to others. Eventually you may decide that you need to have a particular practice where you work on strengthening your I am and meditating and feel inspired to explore your intuitive abilities and so on ...

What we need to understand is that each stage of our lives leads us into a new aspect of exploration and development. We have new questions, new understandings, new ways of expressing ourselves. This is something that needs to be taught and embraced.

It is the fear of change that keeps us stuck in what we know and are comfortable with. We should be on a constant journey of rediscovering and recreating ourselves as well as learning more about the people around us. It is easy to put ourselves or another in a box and keep saying, 'Either accept me for who I am or find someone else', or 'I know you'. The truth is that we don't really know ourselves let alone anyone else. We have to be courageous enough to keep exploring and discovering what new and mysterious aspects live within us. We need to be conscious enough to recognise them when they show up and allow them to mature.

So if something old is not working for you, rejoice and commence the journey towards fresh and extraordinary discoveries.

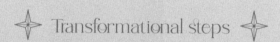

✦ Transformational steps ✦

Reflect on an area in your life that you need to work on. Ask yourself: with the wisdom that I have now, what new possibilities can I embrace in my healing journey? What new thing am I ready to learn and apply? What aspect of my divine inner feminine and masculine self am I ready to connect to and discover that can lead me to the next step of my journey?

ANCESTRAL HEALING, SEXUALITY, AND WHAT'S NEXT

Family patterns and their impact

I f we look at the theme of how we carry our ancestral or family patterns in our bodies, we would have to explore our abilities to digest our life experiences as well as anything that our kin have not faced or healed which has been passed down to us.

We may develop stomach issues based on old emotions and traumas which have not been transformed, leaving the stomach full of the old with no room for anything new.

We could also become stuck in old, fearful patterns of failure, procrastination and not feeling good enough, feeding limitations and in particular worry.

Controlling our environment and those around us is another way our stomach becomes overwhelmed and blocked.

Teeth could also become an issue as we try to process old family guilt, anger, blame and bitterness.

Our skin can become irritated when we feel alone, unprotected, isolated, critical and devalued – especially by those we look up to.

Our intestines can develop obstructions when we feel vulnerable, confused, angry, want to hide and push things away and when we feel that we are different from everyone else.

Our hips can weaken when there are family disagreements, secrets and when we carry others on our hips; as well as holding onto feelings of deception, alienation, too much responsibility, manipulation and strain.

✦ Transformational steps ✦

Create a map for yourself in order to become more conscious of all the layers and areas that need attention based on what you have picked up from your ancestors. Become aware of the threads. Which patterns are similar? Start to work on those first.

To change deeply ingrained patterns in your etheric body takes time, patience, perseverance and self-forgiveness. Work with the process for healing your body at the end of this book.

Exploring ancestral impact

This is such a difficult thing to explore as it's so confrontational to truly see how we have taken on both positive, but in particular, let's call them shadowy, unrefined aspects of our parents' behaviour.

What's most interesting is that even if you haven't spent much time with a parent you could still be acting out their behaviour unconsciously.

And so much of it can be unconscious – especially if you've lived with them. It's often also not the obvious parent – the one you may consider has hurt you the most, whose behaviour may be oozing out of you.

These behaviours might include being pushy and controlling, needing to be right, being manipulative without realising it, being needy and playing the victim. It could involve feelings of being trapped, unseen, misunderstood. It could manifest as an absolute lack of boundaries and respect for self and others, constant worry about things that don't matter, being in a perpetual state of tension, fear of taking steps forward and of change, guilt, self-sabotage, procrastination, or a lack of consideration as to what actions might be healthy and what might be hurtful.

It could mean you treat your partner, children or people close to you in a similar manner (even though you think it's different) to how your parent(s) treated you, recreating from one perspective or another the home environment you had when you were younger, in particular how you felt in this environment or a lack of self-esteem and love similar to that which your parents may have felt. You might create similar money situations or if it's different, you could become either totally obsessed about money or spend it without thinking about it and so on – there are many variations of this. Are you doing what you consider to be different, only to realise it's the same?

One of the most difficult to see or understand is being selfish and extremely self-focused because so many aspects of the inner child are still unrecognised and hiding this part by overworking or overdoing things for others. By energetically creating a feeling that I'm the way I am, take it or leave it and I will hold onto this damaged part and spend most of my time focused on how and why things are not working for me leads to you trying to control everything in your life to make you feel better. This is a never-ending cycle of me, me, me and I need help and attention because I was hurt in the past and I'm still hurting so it's about me. (This can also manifest in all sorts of body issues, blood, weight issues and self-hatred covered up by wanting to look good and youthful.)

This self-focus can have many levels and make people constantly recreate a situation where others feel sorry for them and want to help or save them.

I can go on and on, but what I'm really saying is that healing and transformation have many, many layers and to truly make progress you need to understand that this is not a quick fix process but a process of, first and foremost, learning to become more objective rather than judgemental about yourself, and slowly and consciously starting to work on refining the parts of yourself that need to be worked on. No one can do this for you and it takes quite some time.

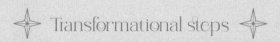

✦ Transformational steps ✦

Start to slowly and gently create a picture and a feeling of how you would love to be. Acknowledge every time you take hold of an old pattern and don't allow it to act out but consciously choose something different. When you are exploring who you would love to be, a great question to contemplate is who would I have been if I had never been hurt? Another powerful question is: what can I learn and then embrace from the hardest moments of my life to become more of who I desire to be? For example, you really wanted to say something hurtful to your partner who did something different to what you wanted them to do but you breathed through it and chose to be kind instead! This is progress. Obviously, every situation is different but you can only change when you have clarity about what kind of a person you would like to be. Sometimes it can take years to unravel who you actually are deep within and often you will find yourself surprisingly different to the roles you took on!

Ancestral healing

nything that your parents, grandparents or great grandparents didn't work on in their mental, emotional and energetic levels is stored in your etheric body, which is also the body of habits.

When one person in the family decides to work on deep family patterns – which can come out as certain diseases, physical weaknesses, emotional challenges such as constant stress, worry, guilt, fear and anxiety mental beliefs about lack and limitations, certain patterns of behaviour, relationship issues – everyone in the family benefits. So just know that when you are willing to go deep you are not just freeing yourself but many others.

I had an amazing experience with my grandfather many years ago. He was in a work camp in Siberia from 14 to 24 years of age. His stories of survival were atrocious yet his intuition and courage is absolutely inspiring.

Around the age of 70 it all started catching up with him and he became depressed, critical and negative to a point that it was difficult to speak to him. One day he was sharing the details of his story with me and it made me quite emotional. This upset him and he stopped sharing as expressing his feelings was not something he or my grandmother were comfortable with. I told him I had to leave, drove home and got into the shower and started crying.

I've never cried like this before; it was equivalent to howling and I knew they were not my tears. I had visions of my grandfather as an emancipated child. So I sent love to him and told him that he could express his feelings through me. (When he was in the work camp no one in his family had any idea whether he was alive or not.)

I wailed like this for an hour. After, I continued sending love and all the beautiful qualities that I felt that part of my grandfather needed.

The next day I called him and carefully said hello, waiting for an onslaught of negativity. But he was completely different: brighter, more alive, happier and more positive. Everyone noticed a huge change in him over the next few weeks and months. It was so heart-warming to be able to work on this huge family trauma and lighten it.

We can all help ourselves and our family by recognising what someone hasn't allowed themselves to feel and having the courage to feel it. You can't push away, cut or suppress that type of energy. It will come out in some way or another until you work with it.

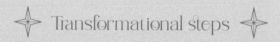

✦ Transformational steps ✦

I encourage you to work with the ancestral release process at the end of this book.

Intuition and sexuality – two paths to follow

I t's fascinating how in our modern world we have managed to connect sexuality with spirituality.

On one hand it can make total sense to view that aspect of our life in a more sacred way, yet on the other hand if and when one learns the higher laws of spirituality it dawns on you how this mixture can lead to major confusion. After all, when we pass over we no longer have sexual organs.

If we look at our present day existence we can see that certain aspects of sexuality have gone out of control. At present it is beamed at us from every direction. The act itself has become a form of gross entertainment. There is no longer a real incentive for deeper connection or honour of your own body or self let alone the development of love.

In fact, we have moved from the possibility of a sacred experience of love to let's just do what animals do. (Not saying this is how every person experiences this, but more and more there is a loss of any kind of real connection and a deep sharing.) It's just become all about pleasure and if you are into developing that, then there are countless practices of various breath techniques and sensual activities to enhance how much pleasure you can experience.

So where does this lead? From observation, usually it leads to more and more desire for pleasure. From a lot of study and experience I believe pleasure that is only for oneself does not lead to evolution! This is a huge conversation as we can use pleasure to awaken our inner being and open our hearts, but it needs to be used for higher good or it becomes another addiction.

How does this connect to our intuition? Well, there are two ways of awakening it. One, through the lower sexual chakras. This often occurs when the focus of our awakening of intuition is selfish and fixated on what we can get out of it, how we can use it to make money and how we can access it with very little effort.

This type of intuition – which is used more often than not – lacks any real refinement, discernment or finesse. It comes from an ancient aspect of ourselves and when awakened and used unconsciously can eventually lead to a moral, emotional, mental and eventually physical breakdown. (I'm talking from both experience of awakening this aspect in myself and seeing it in countless others.)

If you highly value your intuition and it's awakened from very little effort, you are likely to be in this category. In ancient terms it's called atavistic clairvoyance.

The idea is that we need to move it out of the past, which the lower chakras hold and into the future for the development of our higher aspects.

This is why I have some discomfort when people start talking about going into the past and activating old abilities. Not only does it not make sense for evolution but is also quite dangerous and damaging.

Why are we so obsessed with getting something for nothing? Why don't we want to develop the deep joy that one can receive from truly doing the work and paying your dues to gain an ability because you put an appropriate amount of effort into things?

There is no evolution without effort. Just a decline of our higher, nobler qualities.

Therefore, what does it require to awaken the finer aspects of our intuition? It requires a focus on the heart and a daily practice of the type of meditation that the most evolved masters who have walked the earth have left us: focused on evolution as opposed to relaxation. It requires an effort to awaken the sleeping petals of our heart chakra. This involves developing a strong understanding of discernment, an intimate insight into higher worlds and the roles of higher beings.

Furthermore your higher organs of intuition awaken through a deeper mastery of self which includes concentration, equanimity, positivity, open-mindedness and so on, as well as an ability to become objective about yourself. (The less objectivity there is, the more likelihood that what you think is your intuition is actually just a stubborn reflection of your lower self.)

I'm sorry to be so blunt with this and burst the bubble that intuition is just a gift that some have and need to do nothing about or that by developing our sexuality in whatever form we gain this gift. Again, remember there is no sensuality in higher worlds so it makes no sense to enter into it by awakening our intuition through this channel. (And I'm not saying here that you should not work on creating an amazing, loving connection with your partner as that is a beautiful gift. It's just not a gift that should be used for extra sensory perceptions – if you desire accuracy.)

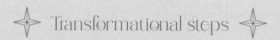

Transformational steps

Do you prefer fast or instant pleasure? Do you take the time to meditate on your experiences and gain wisdom from them?

I encourage you to start practising a process of deeper self-reflection. This will not only improve your concentration but will also help you to start to respond instead of react in life and refine your astral body which then gives you more access to objectivity and intuitive insight.Give yourself 10 minutes a day. Pick a situation where you had been reactive instead of responsive. Remember what occurred when this situation or confrontation ended. Do not judge yourself, just notice your sensations. Keep remembering what occurred as if you are rewinding everything back in time. Each time you notice yourself reacting emotionally – stop, ask what way you could have responded in this scenario and what other choices were available to you. Notice every little detail of what occurred. This simple exercise of self-reflection backwards can help to awaken your higher self.

Trust and judgement

I'd like to explore the idea of trust and judgement.

How can we live in trust that every impactful experience can move us forward? This can only happen if our thinking and feeling life gains humility and delicateness. Then our focus shifts from protecting, limiting and judging to moving forward, discovering and expanding.

Can we take every experience that has somehow touched us and ask: where is this touching my heart? (It is irrelevant whether it is painful or beautiful.)

We also need to stop seeing each other based on someone else's opinion (if I did that I would have no close friends) and on what they were like a year ago, a month ago, even a day ago. (So many times I've had to remind people close to me that I have grown from when we last spoke – which could have been an hour ago. Asking them to be present with me and keep discovering who I am now as opposed to who they are holding on to.)

This is truly one of the most difficult things to do – to discover who someone is in the moment as opposed to holding on to the past. At the same time we have to be aware of deep old patterns and traumas and how they show up. When we understand more about ourselves, we start to have more empathy for others and become more responsive as opposed to reactive.

We don't realise how each criticism creates a stop program. If I've judged someone or have bought into a judgement, I can no longer see the beauty or the humanity of another. I can no longer receive a gift of their heart or their wisdom. Thus, I cannot allow my heart the possibility to be open and trust the process of healing exploration.

What if we could be aware of someone's weaknesses, but delved deeper and worked on discovering what their possibility for growth is, and then encouraged it with gentleness?

What if, instead of being attached, we could observe our judgements and feel what they do to our own body and how they affect another.

We need to be aware that as much as we have opinions about others, we also have pain that they trigger so when a person shares an intimate story of something they are not proud of and we say, 'That's so immature', or use critical words the other person usually feels cut off, guilty, angry and attacked. From there instead of shining their beauty, they hide it with harshness in order to self-protect.

What we don't realise is that the person who made the judgement could have been hurt by something similar and instead of recognising their own pain and an opportunity for healing they judge.

Usually all this leads to physical pain inside the body, especially around the neck, throat, heart, back and digestive system.

So for the person who shared something intimate about themselves, the opportunity is often around learning to create healthy boundaries, listening to their inner wisdom and stop people pleasing.

For the person who has judged the possibility is to recognise the triggers and look at what has happened in their past which was hurtful and work on loving and healing their inner child and listening to their heart again.

When we are open-minded and willing to explore and self-reflect we have a possibility of transformation. This doesn't mean we have no discernment just that we explore as opposed to block and we learn to trust ourselves.

✦ Transformational steps ✦

Become conscious of when you criticise – this could be yourself and others. Start to develop a practice of seeing the blessings in imperfections. Each time a judgement occurs in your mind, ask how you can see this person or situation from a place of kindness and wisdom.

I also encourage you to work with the trauma release, shadow and forgiveness processes at the end of this book.

Where to from here?

Fear, hatred, judgement and doubt harden our I or sense of self. The more we feed those qualities, the more we start to believe that every individual is only in it for themselves and we can become locked into our personalities.

Egoism occurs when we deny our higher faculties of goodness and stay in self-involvement, which always leads to feelings of isolation and separation.

Whenever we embark on the train of thought that 'nobody understand me' we immediately limit our development. Yet, feeling separated is also a very necessary part of evolution.

So is this suffering that we all seem to experience really necessary? Unfortunately, it appears that a huge number of humanity only wake up to what is going on both in their inner being as well as the world when they experience pain. Yet it is possible to grow from love, kindness, joy and awareness.

From my study I have learned that God or the source is always evolving by creating new beings who have new capacities, who in turn create new beings, who again have new capacities.

Where does it end?

It doesn't.

Where did it begin?

I can only imagine that source had the intention to bring something completely new into the cosmos – a free loving human race.

We are the beings of freedom and love. Yet freedom requires us to choose by seeing both love and hate, fear and courage, judgement and acceptance, war and peace and deciding which one we are going to feed.

When we first started to incarnate, we really didn't fathom how difficult it would be to split away from the source; however, through the power of our I and the warmth of our heart we can overcome fear, hatred, judgement and doubt and can then awaken our capacity for compassion, forgiveness and love.

We have the monumental task to develop our own will to match that of the divine. This is a huge experiment and will take us many incarnations to fulfil. Can we evolve from taking to giving, which is the order of evolution?

The good news is that we have help.

✦ Transformational steps ✦

Reflect on your life so far. What choices have you made that you are proud of? What choices did you make that you wish you hadn't? What was the basis of each choice, for instance, did you make it from fear of lack or from your desire to contribute?

Work with strengthening your I am process from the back of the book then take some time to reflect on what freedom means to you.

Processes that can help you grow

This section is all about working with processes that can help you experience the deepest transformation possible. Every time you do the processes you will gain more insights from them. For deeper transformation I encourage you to check out my online courses www.innasegal.com

Things to be aware of when you do any of the processes:

★ Be open-minded, breathe slowly and deeply and do not judge.

★ Any insight is a good insight.

★ If you have a pen and paper next to you and you feel you need to write something down, please do so. Ideally you should regularly work with a journal.

★ Be willing to explore and ask questions.

★ Imagine a purple fire in front of you and with your hands take charged energy out of your body and place it in the fire. At the end of the process put out the fire.

★ Be willing to take responsibility and make changes in your life.

★ It's important that you do something, even if it's a small positive action, within 48 hours of doing the processes.

TRANSFORMATIONAL PROCESSES FOR PHYSICAL, EMOTIONAL AND ANCESTRAL HEALING

Process for
healing your body

onnect to a particular part of your body and breathe into it. Allow yourself to enter into the pain or discomfort and explore.

Ask yourself: if this pain had a shape, what shape would it be? Angular and sharp or circular and stifling? What is the surface of the discomfort? Is it smooth or abrasive?

What is the colour of this pain? If the pain had a voice, what would it say? Allow it to speak.

What point of view does the pain have on your life?

When did the pain begin? Did it first start from an emotional, mental, energetic or physical point of view?

Where in your body did it originally begin? Place your hands on that part of your body.

What was the message that it wanted you to understand?

Where you able to listen?

What process did this painful message go through to build and become what it is now?

Now imagine sitting in front of a purple fire – what old and outdated ideas are you able to let go of? Place them into the fire.

Once you feel you have let go of as much as possible, shake your body as vigorously as you can without hurting yourself then take a step forward.

What is a new, healing point of view that you can take on?

What colour does it have? Breathe it in.

What are the qualities that the colour possesses that you need to receive?

Can you feel any new energy or vitality awaken?

Place your hands on that part of your body. Acknowledge it and expand it.

Ask: what actions do I need to take daily to be pain free?

What do I need to do to take a step towards healing the condition I have?

What would it be like to have no pain or sickness and to have a sense of strength, connection and well-being?

Allow these insights to assimilate in your inner being.

Take a few moments to assimilate those possibilities.

Feel the strength which awakens within you.

Slowly open your eyes.

Work with this process daily.

To heal and transform your life you must develop a strong sense of self-love and self-care.

This is a really powerful process to work on that.

Self-love process

sk yourself: what does self-love mean to me?

If there was a cup inside me with healing liquid that would demonstrate my level of self-love and care how full or empty would it be?

If this cup had a colour, what colour would it be? Is this a healthy colour for me?

If this cup is empty, ask: how do I refill it? Is it by trying to get some love, care, attention and acknowledgement from others or is it through food, clothes, work, emotions, TV, media and so on?

How is this working for you? Does it nourish you or does it deplete you more?

Does that create more neediness in you and an addiction for that type of nourishment or do you try to develop a true practice of self-connection?

Does this practice contain time for self-reflection, connection with nature, rest, meditation, dance or movement, emotional sharing, healing, creativity, touch, reading, learning love, tenderness, open-heartedness, development of your inner confidence and connection to the divine?

Does this practice make you more sensitised and aware on a daily basis?

If you do not have a practice, what can you start to do daily that can open your heart?

If you do have a practice, how can you enhance it so that every time you feel empty or down, you do something to strengthen yourself?

Remember: every time you fall and get up, you end up strengthening your inner being.

Place your hands on your heart. Breathe into your heart and soften it. Imagine that a beautiful, yellow ray of warmth and softness is now being poured into your heart – breathe it in allowing yourself to receive it fully. How good are you at receiving it and allowing your heart to soften?

Do not judge, just allow. Now imagine a soft, peach ray of light coming into your heart and awakening your creativity. Allow it to revitalise your heart and enliven it. Do not add anything outside of yourself to it. Just allow it to enliven it. Now ask what other colour your heart needs and what it is related to and allow yourself to receive it.

Every time you want to connect to someone else for your nourishment tune into your inner cup and ask: am I fully in myself or am I trying to fill myself up with someone else's energy?

How do I fill myself first as a practice before I reach out to someone else or something else? What qualities am I trying to get from the other person or that other thing that I can offer to myself first? (Is it acceptance, strength, kindness, gratitude, love?)

Work with the colours or one of your practices then explore as your cup gets filled. From that space connect to that person or people or things. How does that feel? Can you create a practice of filling yourself up first and then connecting to others?

Imagine yourself doing this. Acknowledge yourself for the time you are taking to give to you now. Ask: what am I willing to practice in the next day and next week that will strengthen me?

Slowly come back.

Trauma release process

We have all experienced difficult or traumatic occurrences in our lives. This process can help you to identify a challenging experience and then work on turning it around into something empowering and strengthening.

Find a quiet place to sit, stand or lie down.

Connect to your body. Take slow, deep breaths and become aware of where in your body there is discomfort. Allow yourself to really explore the feeling.

Is it heavy, tight, cold or sharp?

If it looked like a shape, what shape would it be? A triangle, a square, a circle?

If this trauma had a colour, what colour would it be?

If this part of you had an age, would it be an old, ancient part of you or a young part of you?

If this part had a voice, what would it say?

If this aspect was connected to a particular memory, what would it be?

If you could determine the point of view you took on from that experience, what would it be?

Imagine a purple fire in front of you. Place any pain, heavy charge and discomfort from this part of your body into the purple flame.

Now ask yourself: what is something valuable that I could learn from this difficult experience? Allow it to rise up inside of you.

What would be a colour that is related to this new point of view? Imagine being completely bathed by this colour. Breathe it in, feel it.

Ask: how can I use what happened for my greatest good and the greatest good of all those who I care about?

Imagine using this experience to make a positive difference in your life and others. Use this colour to move you forward. Create a gesture with your hands that can remind you of the empowered possibilities that you can focus on.

Then come back to the present.

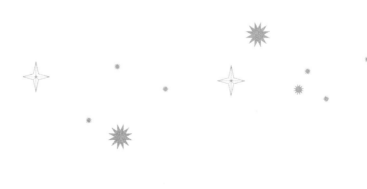

Strengthening your I am process

T his process helps you to reflect on your day and on different events that you have experienced and to become more objective. This strengthens your sense of self and your I am and allows you to start taking charge of your behaviour.

Find a quiet place to sit, stand or lie down. Take some slow breaths in and relax your stomach muscles.

To strengthen your I, pick a recent memory which has emotions or charge attached to it.

Place your hands on your solar plexus. Find detail in the memory, faces, colours and textures.

Try and see yourself in the picture like you would see the others involved. Separate your mind's eye and see the image of yourself acting out in the memory.

What are you doing in this memory?

Feelings might be coming up; this is normal at this stage.

Be objective and ask: what is making me act in this way? Is it the other person, the environment, the mood? Am I tired and hungry?

Now move the memory backwards, starting from the end of what happened and moving through to the beginning. Your goal is to see yourself and the other parties involved in the memory without attaching too many personal feelings to it.

To do this you have to overcome your guilt or whatever emotions are playing out and see this situation with a detachedness that opens your capacity to be objective. You need to see yourself in the memory as you would see a friend telling you a story of his or her own sufferings then you can counsel yourself on how you could have behaved better.

Now imagine yourself acting in a different manner. Let the memory be changed with your new behaviour. Try one more way you could have acted instead of the original memory.

Bring yourself back to the present.

This is very powerful as it frees the I from the subjectivity of the astral body and elevates you into a higher state of being.

This inner retrospective reflection should be practised every night to strengthen the I.

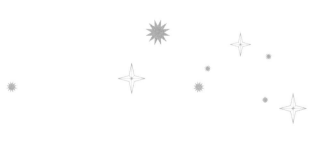

Ancestral release process

We have all taken on beliefs, behaviours and points of view from our family. This process will help you to start to release old ancestral patterns and take powerful steps forward as well as to discern what you are carrying is yours, as opposed to what you took on from your tribe.

Stand up, shake your body for 40-60 seconds.

Imagine a see-through red light moving from your feet up your legs, back, shoulders, head and to the front of your body. Become aware of where the energy becomes stuck.

Take a few moments to explore which part of your body is holding on to this old energy.

Ask yourself: what is in my ancestral history that needs attention now? What are some repetitive patterns that I have seen people in my family play out and I have taken on?

Breathe and allow a thought, a feeling, an image or a memory to show up.

If this old energy had a shape, what would it be? If it had a colour, what colour would it be? If it had a voice, what would it say?

What does this pattern do to you? Does it block you? Does it pull you back into the past? Does it make you play a victim? Does it criticise you? Does it make you small? Does it make you angry?

Feel it, listen to it and face it.

Become aware, if you haven't already, who is the person or people in your family that are or were holding this energy?

See them in front of you.

Reflect on what the learning opportunity is that they are offering you.

Say: I thank you for the learning which I am embracing, I no longer choose to feed, participate in, or lose my energy to the negative aspect of this pattern.

Now imagine a purple fire in front of you.

Connect back to the shape and the colour of this energy. Start to separate what you need to learn from what you need to let go of. Take out anything that you are ready to let go of. Become aware of the behaviour and how you play it out.

Do you speak in the same way as one of your parents – with the same tone of voice, using the same words?

Do you hold back and not say things that are important to say?

Do you sit on the fence or are you in conflict with others?

Take any of this out of your body; shake it out.

Every time you are feeling stuck become aware of how you stop breathing and start tensing then acknowledge it and take it out.

Know that this is a process you will need to repeat regularly.

Now focus on the opportunity of strength and self-love that you can give yourself.

What is the colour of it?

How can you embrace it?

What new healing opportunity does it offer?

How can this build your self-worth and strength?

Allow a few moments to assimilate this experience and then come back to the present.

Shadow process

T he shadow can be viewed as painful, unprocessed parts of ourselves that have the potential to hinder many aspects of our lives at the most inappropriate moments and when we are least prepared.

When you disown your shadow you embark on a journey of fear, guilt, anger, possible illness and separation. When you embrace your shadow you are on a path to experiencing wholeness and healing.

Close your eyes. Take some deep breaths in and out. Become aware of the part of you that sabotages things in your life. This could be as simple as being late for your appointments or not allowing yourself to heal, eat healthy, create new business opportunities or open your heart to your current partner or a new relationship or friendship.

If this part could take on a shape of an archetypal character, what would it look like? Would it be tall and overweight, thin and ethereal or something in between?

If this part had a voice, what would it say? What is the reason this part wants to sabotage or hurt you?

Is there a feeling of guilt, shame or anger connected to this shadow aspect?

Listen to this part while taking deep breaths in and out. Feel whatever feelings or sensations arise.

Imagine a purple flame in front of you. With your hands take out any charge from your body and place it into the purple fire.

Say: I let go, I let go, I let go.

Thank this shadow part.

Ask yourself: what is it that I gain from self-sabotaging myself? Is it that I have an excuse for judging, blaming and criticising others and life? Does self-sabotaging give me the power to self-hate and then self-punish?

What behaviour have I made okay that I am ready to change?

What would happen if I took radical responsibility for my life? What if I was willing to embrace and befriend my shadow by seeing it, understanding it and learning from it?

Stand up. Place your hands on your heart. Ask to listen to and follow your heart's wisdom with true courage. Imagine taking full responsibility for your life and take a moment to reflect on what that means to you.

Do you need to talk to someone and take accountability for your behaviour and what you said you will do?

Do you need to forgive someone?

Do you need to stop procrastinating and start taking action?

What positive change are you willing to make?

Give yourself permission to move forward.

What is the new feeling in your body?

What are you willing to do in the next 48 hours towards this transformation?

Take a moment to feel it and bring it into your heart, knowing that you can embrace your shadow and transform your life.

Forgiveness process

P lace your hands on your heart. Ask your deepest heart: where is there still a charge, where is there still hidden blame, resentment or anger in my being over a difficult event? Who are the individuals involved? Choose one person.

Try and go beyond anything you have ever thought of before as you consider the exchange between this person and yourself.

Did this person teach you how to have healthy boundaries?

Did they teach you how to communicate more lovingly and treat others with more respect?

Did they teach you how to have more humility and use your power to help rather than to hurt?

Did they teach you how to be compassionate and selfless?

Did they show you a type of darkness you yourself may have perpetrated in a previous life and that you are now working to transform?

Stay with this until you come up with a deeper understanding. If you are stuck move your body and attempt to see the situation from a higher perspective.

How can this person and experience be assisting you to understand your karma? Remember that everything has a meaning and every event is in your life to help you grow.

What are the possible ways that you have grown or can grow because of this difficult experience? Remember that we slowly learn how to be more noble people over many lives. Through all our suffering something in us is purified.

Now feel your heart and open it. Imagine this person is in front of you. Check into your body to feel any new sensations with this person in front of you.

Say: I understand that you are an important part of my lessons in this life. I thank you for teaching me

_____

(take your time to say what it is they have taught you.)

I now choose to take responsibility for learning the lessons that are part of my soul destiny. (What does it mean for you to take responsibility and not blame anyone else? How would you grow if every time you thought of this person you focused not on what they did, but on what they were teaching you?)

Imagine taking on new perceptions and behaviours. See yourself reacting to your loved ones in a new way based on what this person has taught you.

What else is this person teaching you that can make you grow?
Say: as I grow in strength I will let go of my

_____

(say what it is, for instance, anger, hatred, frustration)

and I will develop more

_____

(compassion, objectivity, love and so on).

With time I will free you and free myself from this painful experience.
With time I will forgive you and I will grow. With time I will hold
a new picture of you and you will have the possibility to heal and grow.

If possible, send some appreciation to this person to whatever
degree you can. If this soul is still suffering in darkness separate the
human side of them and send extra love towards them.

You know that you have completely let go of charge when you can
think of this person and experience understanding and gratitude.

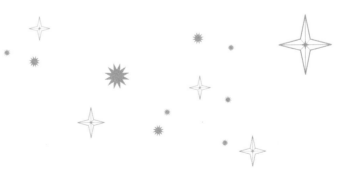

Conclusion

The idea of this book arose from the posts I shared on social media over a few years, where I desired to shake people out of their internal slumber and encourage them to ask deeper questions, think for themselves and grow!

Through the exploration of the various topics I have included in this book, I encourage you to take the time to tune in, think deeply and discover what is possible.

Developing our inner life has been greatly underrated by society, as it is something that lots of people do not understand and thus do not value. Instead, outer success and money are seen as an emblem of high accomplishment while we are here on earth. Please understand I am not saying that co-creating abundance is not important or useful in our life experience. What I am saying is that there are deeper riches which we need to explore in order to allow our soul and spirit to expand and gain the depth and the wisdom that we came here to experience.

I deeply encourage you to not only read the ideas I have shared in this book but to also regularly and diligently work with the healing processes and the transformational steps I have included.

I encourage you to write all your insights and observations in a journal.

I wish you all the best on your journey of exploring your soul and higher truths!

Acknowledgements

This book was inspired by my many years of learning, teaching and doing one on one healing sessions in various countries.

In the last decade I have been incredibly stirred by the teachings of Rudolf Steiner. I have approached his teachings with an open mind, and have spent thousands of hours reading, exploring, attending courses, connecting the various pieces of the puzzle together and having profound discussions with wonderful teachers. Most of all I have tried to decipher the great relevance of Anthroposophical teachings in our present day lives.

I encourage anyone who is ready to stretch their mind, heart and soul to explore the teachings of Rudolf Steiner. Just make sure you take it one little step at a time with the awareness that much of his work is over a hundred years old but is still incredibly profound and relevant. My advice is to start with his book Theosophy before jumping into his deeper work.

I want to thank my wonderful family: my beautiful children, parents and partner for their love, encouragement and for constantly giving me an opportunity to keep growing and evolving.

I am grateful to Lisa and Paul at Rockpool Publishing, for their continual, encouragement and support! Thank you from the bottom of my heart.

Also thank you to Brooke Halliwell for your help with editing and Sara Lindberg for your beautiful design.

And of course, I am incredibly grateful to you, the reader, for being willing to explore this book. May your soul become deeply enriched and your life full of colour!

Love Inna